Concise
Handbook
of
English
Composition

A
Concise
Handbook
of
English
Composition

L. HUGH MOORE

Georgia Institute of Technology

KARL F. KNIGHT

Old Dominion University

Prentice-Hall, Inc., *Englewood Cliffs, New Jersey*

ISBN: 0-13-166959-1

Library of Congress Catalog Card Number: 71-38717

10 9 8 7 6 5 4 3 2 1

Printed in the United States of America

PRENTICE-HALL INTERNATIONAL, INC., London
PRENTICE-HALL OF AUSTRALIA, PTY. LTD., Sydney
PRENTICE-HALL OF CANADA, LTD., Toronto
PRENTICE-HALL OF INDIA PRIVATE LIMITED, New Delhi
PRENTICE-HALL OF JAPAN, INC., Tokyo

Preface

We now know that teaching "rules" of grammar and rhetoric does little to raise the quality of student writing. Yet most teachers of English feel a need to have some source of essential information on grammar, punctuation, diction, composition, and rhetoric to which to refer the student without overwhelming him with discussion and examples. *A Concise Handbook of English Composition* attempts to deal succinctly with the most frequent problems students encounter in writing for college courses. Avoiding a rigidly prescriptive approach, this book offers straightforward, understandable suggestions to improve writing. These suggestions range from the punctuation of a sentence to the composition of a research paper. Effectiveness of communication is the goal in each case.

A Concise Handbook of English Composition is designed primarily as a handbook, not a textbook. Its brevity should result in the student using it more frequently and effectively than he might a longer textbook. For the instructor it provides an easy-to-use tool to indicate to the student what needs to be changed and how to go about making the necessary revisions. The contents are in a readily usable form: the text is keyed to the symbols in common use by English teachers; the Table of Contents is detailed, the Index exhaustive; and the running heads allow the user to locate information by simply thumbing through the pages.

This book recognizes that students still need help with their writing, help that lengthy discussions may not provide. And it recognizes that a handbook can be a valuable timesaver for the teacher. This *Concise Handbook* gives essential guidance for the writing, correction, and revision of student papers, guidance which might be used profitably in many courses other than freshman composition.

Correction Symbols

ab	abbreviation (MS 7)	*emph*	emphasis (SS 6c)
adj	adjective (GR 12)	*ex*	exactness (D 6)
adv	adverb (GR 12)	*fig*	figurative language (D 13) (Log 7)
agr/sv	agreement of subject and verb (GR 4)	*fn*	footnote (MS 5)
agr/p	agreement of pronoun and antecedent (GR 5)	*frag*	sentence fragment (GR 3)
		gl	glossary of usage (Chapter 10)
ambig	ambiguous (Log 2)	*gr*	grammar (Chapter 3)
apos	apostrophe (Sp 1)	*hyp*	hyphen (Sp 2)
awk	awkward	*id*	idiom (D 11)
bibl	bibliography (LP 2) (MS 5)	*inc*	incomplete (GR 13)
C	comma (P 2)	*inv*	awkward inversion
cap	capitalization (Sp 4)	*ital*	italics (MS 6)
case	case (GR 7)	*jar*	jargon (D 8)
CF	comma fault (GR 1)	*lc*	lower case (Sp 4)
cl	clause (SS 4)	*leg*	legibility
coh	coherence (Par 2)	*len*	sentence length (SS 6c) paragraph length (Par 3)
colloq	colloquial (D 1b)		
compl	complement (SS 2e)	*log*	logic (Chapter 9)
compr	comparison of adjective and adverb (GR 12d) (Log 3)	*LP*	library paper (Chapter 7)
		mm	misplaced modifier (GR 11)
con	connective (SS 2c)	*mod*	modifier (SS 2a)
coord	coordination (SS 4)	*mech*	mechanics (MS)
CS	comma splice (GR 1)	*MS*	manuscript mechanics (Chapter 8)
dial	dialect (D 3)		
dgl	dangling modifier (GR 9)	*mx*	mixed metaphor (Log 7) (D 13)
det	details (Log 4) (Log 5)		
ec	economy (SS 6a)	*nr*	numbers (MS 9)

obj	object (SS 2f)	*U*	unity (Par 1)
outl	outline (LP 4)	*usage*	level of usage (D 1)
P	punctuation (Chapter 4)	*V*	vague (Log 6)
pag	pagination (MS 2)	*var*	sentence variety (SS 6c)
par	parallelism (SS 6b)		paragraph variety (Par 3)
pass	passive voice (SS 6a) (GR 8b)	*WC*	word choice (D)
phr	phrase (SS 3)	*WO*	word order
pl	plural (Sp 3)	*WW*	wrong word (D)
QM	question mark (P 5)	?	clarity (Log)
ref	pronoun reference (GR 6)	ℐ	delete
rep	awkward repetition (SS 6)	⌣	join
	(D 7)	//	parallel structure (SS 6b)
run-on	run-on sentence (GR 2)	#	separate
SC	semicolon (P 3)	*tr*	transpose
shift	shift in tense, mood, person,	¶	paragraphing (Chapter 2)
	or voice (GR 8)	○	delete the circled punctuation
sl	slang (D 2)	·/	add period (P 1)
sp	spelling (Chapter 5)	,/	add comma (P 2)
sq	squinting construction	;/	add semicolon (P 3)
	(GR 10)	:/	add colon (P 4)
SS	sentence error (Chapter 1)	?/	add question mark (P 5)
stil	stilted language (D 9)	!/	add exclamation point (P 6)
sub	subordination (SS 4)	−/	add dash (P 7)
SV	sentence variety (SS 6)	"/	add quotation marks (P 8)
syl	syllabification (Sp 2c) (MS 8)		(MS 1) (MS 3)
T	tense of verb (GR 8c)	()/	add parentheses (P 9)
trans	transition (Par 2)	[ ] /	add brackets (P 10) (MS 3e)
trite	trite expression (D 10)	=/	add hyphen

Contents

3 GRAMMAR (Gr)   25

4 PUNCTUATION (P)   43

5 SPELLING (Sp)   51

6 DICTION AND STYLE (D)   63

7 LIBRARY PAPERS (LP)   70

8 MECHANICS OF MANUSCRIPTS (MS)   75

9 LOGIC AND CLARITY (Log)   88

10 GLOSSARY OF USAGE (Gl)   97

1

Sentences

SS

Classified according to purpose, a sentence is a declaration (makes a statement), a question, a command or request, or an exclamation (expresses feeling or emphasizes fact). It is punctuated as an independent unit ending with a period, question mark, or exclamation point. A sentence is constructed from one or more of the eight parts of speech:

VERBS express action or being. (Asimov *writes* novels. He *is* a scientist.)

NOUNS name persons, places, things, ideas, qualities, and actions. (*San Francisco* is a lovely *city*.)

PRONOUNS take the place of nouns. (*He* was obsessed with *her*.)

ADJECTIVES modify nouns and pronouns. (*Polluted* rivers, *poisonous* air, and *denuded* forests are all too *common*.)

ADVERBS modify verbs, adjectives, other adverbs, verbals, phrases, clauses, or the rest of the sentence. (Time passes *very swiftly*.)

PREPOSITIONS relate their noun or pronoun object to the rest of the sentence. (Violent men are filled *with* rage.)

CONJUNCTIONS act as connectors. (Subtlety *and* ambiguity characterize many modern novels, *but* most readers prefer simple tales.)

INTERJECTIONS are words or phrases like *Ouch*! An interjection may be any part of speech.

The parts of speech in a sentence are sentence elements: subjects, verbs, modifiers, connectives, complements, and objects.

SS 1 • *Basic Components: Subject and Verb*

Almost all sentences have a subject and a verb. The subject may be a noun, pronoun, noun clause, gerund, or infinitive. The simple subject is a single word; the complete subject is the simple subject and its modifiers.

The verb is plural if the subject is plural; it is singular if the subject is singular; and it expresses time relationship (tense). In declarative sentences the verb normally follows the subject; in questions it usually precedes the subject. The verb identifies the action performed by the subject, the basic relationship in the sentence. Participles, gerunds, and infinitives cannot be used as complete verbs. The predicate is the verb with its related words—objects, complements, and modifiers.

Verbs are:

transitive (they require an object to complete the action).

$$s \qquad\quad v \qquad\qquad o$$
The *ground crew laid* the new *Astro Turf* with great care.

intransitive (they require no object).

$$s \quad v \qquad\qquad\; \text{adv. phr.}$$
Motionless, the *iguanas lay* basking *in the fierce sun.*

linking (they connect the subject to a noun or adjective).

$$s \qquad\qquad\qquad lv \qquad \text{pred. adj.}$$
Byron's *use* of forced rhyme *is* very *skillful.*

Only a few sentences are complete without subjects and verbs:

Commands and requests usually have *you* as an understood subject.

"Send not to ask for whom the bell tolls."

Verbs are not always needed in exclamations, short answers, or some descriptions.

What a shot! Not bad for an amateur. Good distance, right direction, perfect position.

SS 2 • *Additional Elements of the Sentence*

a. *Modifiers* describe, qualify, or limit other sentence elements. Modifiers may be words (adjectives or adverbs), phrases, or clauses. Typically, a modifier describes a subject, complement, or other modifier or tells why, where, when, or how the action occurred.

adj.

The Voyage of the Beagle is an *exciting* book.

adv.

Darwin wrote *well.*

adj.   adj.

The *outrageous* Oscar Wilde enunciated *noble* truths.

adv. adv.

Next he *calmly* waved a lily.

Phrases or clauses that modify main elements function as adjectives or adverbs.

After Schliemann read Homer, he was determined to find Troy. (Adverbial phrase tells when and modifies *was determined.*)

b. *Appositives* are nouns or their equivalent that supplement the meaning of other nouns. Appositives are restrictive if they limit the noun they modify to a particular [Jack the Giant Killer] or nonrestrictive if they merely add more information [Alexander Wilson, the father of American ornithology]. Adjectives with phrases may sometimes function as adjectival appositives.

She finally completed her book, *elegant and heavy with details and digressions.* (Adjectival appositive.)

c. *Connectives* join sentence elements; they include three types:

Coordinating conjunctions (and, or, nor, for, but, so, yet) join two equal elements.

Industrial pollution threatens our entire environment, *but* the public remains apathetic.

Subordinating conjunctions (such as after, although, because, before, if, since, so, until, when, where, while) join a subordinate element to the main clause.

Because industrial pollution is steadily increasing, public action is urgently needed.

Transitional conjunctions (such as therefore, however, thus, consequently) join two main clauses by providing a link between them and are preceded by a mark stronger than a comma.

> Control of industrial pollution is urgently needed; *however,* the public seems not to care.

d. *Prepositions*, another type of connective, relate a noun or pronoun to the basic sentence elements, so that the prepositional phrase functions adjectivally or adverbially.

> He scored *with impunity*. [The phrase functions adverbially, modifying *scored*.]
>
> The British commonly drink whisky *without ice*. [The phrase functions adjectivally, modifying *whisky*.]

The *relative pronouns who, which,* and *that* connect adjective clauses to the basic sentence elements.

> The pilot *who chased the saucer* never returned.

e. *Complements* are nouns or adjectives (called predicate nouns or predicate adjectives) that complete or describe the subject. A complement is connected to its subject by a copula or linking word [*to be, seem, appear,* and, sometimes, *feel, grow, look, smell, taste,* and *sound*].

>   pn
> *Little Big Man* is a fine western *novel*. (*Novel* is a predicate noun.)
>   pa
> It seems absolutely *authentic*. (*Authentic* is a predicate adjective.)
>   lv   pa
> I *feel awful* (linking verb, predicate adjective).
>   o
> I always *feel* my *forehead* to see if I am feverish (nonlinking, action verb, takes an object).

f. *Objects* are of several types. The direct object of a verb is a noun or pronoun, usually following the verb. It names the recipient of the action which the verb describes. The direct object answers the questions "what?" or "whom?"

>   v   do
> Jack Johnson *won the heavyweight title* from Tommy Burns.

Indirect objects, usually preceding the direct object, occur with verbs of telling, asking, giving, and the like. The indirect object answers the question "*to* what?" or "*to* whom?"

io
Upton Sinclair gave the *Lilly Library* his manuscripts and letters.

Verbals, such as infinitives and participles, may also have objects.

"To see a *world* in a grain of sand."

The object of a preposition is the noun or pronoun which the preposition relates to the rest of the sentence.

op
Lantern fish live near the sea *floor.*

op
Nero Wolfe is abnormally fond of *food.*

SS 3 • *Phrases*

A phrase is a group of two or more related words that does not include a complete subject and predicate. Within a sentence, the words function as nouns, verbs, adjectives, or adverbs.

Verb phrase: We *shall prevail*.
Prepositional phrase: We shall prevail *in the future*.
Gerund phrase: *Reviewing a play* can be nervewracking.
Participial phrase: A critic *reviewing a play* must be perceptive.
Infinitive phrase: He likes *to attend plays*.

Participles, gerunds, and infinitives are verbals. Like verbs, they have tenses and, often, subjects and objects and may be modified by adverbs. Not being complete verbs, they cannot alone make a complete statement.

Types of Phrases

a. *Noun phrases*. Gerund phrases always act as nouns (*Reliving past glory* is a melancholy activity). Infinitive phrases may also serve as nouns (*To know her* is *to love her*) and even, occasionally, so can a prepositional phrase (*Before the First World War* was a bucolic time in England).

b. *Adjective phrases*. Prepositional phrases, infinitive phrases, and participial phrases can act as adjectives.

Her generosity is *of a magnitude* that is barely discernible. (Prepositional phrase becomes a predicate adjective following the linking verb *is*.)

It is delightful to discover a statistic *to prove one's point*. (Infinitive phrase modifies *statistic*.)

Scholars *studying the past* are wary of drawing causal connections. (Participial phrase modifies *scholars*.)

c. *Adverbial phrases.* Prepositional phrases and infinitive phrases may function as adverbs.

Read the Marquis de Sade *with discretion*. (Modifies *read*.)

He is, *to be sure*, controversial. (Modifies the entire sentence.)

d. *Absolute phrases.* Absolute phrases have no grammatical connection to any specific element in the main clause.

His desire to publish his discoveries thwarted, the doctor gave up his research. (Nominative absolute.)

Hell, no, we won't go! (Interjection.)

Please, *ladies and gentlemen*, be seated. (Noun of direct address.)

SS 4 • *Clauses*

Clauses have complete subjects and verbs. Main clauses form the principal grammatical units of the sentence and are complete in themselves. Subordinate clauses serve as nouns, adjectives, or adverbs. They are usually introduced by either subordinating conjunctions (*after, although, as, because, before, if, since, until, when, while*) or relative pronouns (*who, which, that*).

Subordinate clauses as nouns may be introduced by *that, what, whatever, where, wherever, who, whoever, when, whenever, whether*. These clauses are familiar to us in definitions and explanations, where they are complements:

comp.
One of Freud's basic assumptions was *that traumas in childhood have lasting effects*.

As direct objects (their most frequent use):

d.o.
Voltaire attacked *what was unfair or repressive*.

They may be used also as subjects, indirect objects, and objects of prepositions:

s.
Whatever Alfred Hitchcock does in his films is closely analyzed by French directors.

ind. obj.
Antonioni gave *whoever came* a job as an extra in his movie about decadent Rome.

obj. of prep.
Should an author feel responsible for *whether or not his book is honestly advertised?*

Subordinate clauses as adjectives modify a noun, pronoun, or gerund. They usually follow the word they modify and are introduced by a relative pronoun which acts as a subject or object in the clause.

adj.
"These are the times *that try men's souls.*"

adj.
To Shakespeare, a great person *who lacked self-knowledge* courted disaster.

Relative adverbs may also introduce adjective clauses.

rel. adv.
Youth is a time *when all things seem possible.*

Poe is one American writer [whom] *the French greatly admire.*

Subordinate clauses used as adverbs modify adjectives, adverbs, verbals, prepositional phrases, or whole clauses. Depending on the importance of an adverbial clause, it may precede or follow the main clause. Adverb clauses express relationships that involve time, place, direction, cause, effect, condition, manner, or concession.

"*Because I could not stop for death,* He kindly stopped for me."
After Lisbon had been destroyed by the earthquake of 1775, Voltaire rejected Optimism.

Special problems in the use of subordinate clauses:

Avoid stringing together a long, awkward series of dependent clauses.

Awkward: George Plimpton, who is an editor and critic, wrote *The Paper Lion,* which is about professional football, which is one of our major preoccupations and which is good reading for those who appreciate sports.

Better: George Plimpton, an editor and critic, wrote *The Paper Lion* about professional football, one of our major preoccupations. It is good reading for those who appreciate sports.

Avoid seesaw subordination—sentences that begin and end with similar subordinate clauses.

> When Faulkner came to the city he was always unhappy when he had to stay for any length of time.

Avoid inverted subordination: putting the main idea in a subordinate clause.

Inverted: When he contracted tuberculosis (subordinate clause), Keats was very young (main clause).

Improved: Keats contracted tuberculosis (main clause) when he was very young (subordinate clause).

Inverted: When he found that no American car was safe (subordinate clause), Ralph Nader was investigating the automobile industry (main clause).

Improved: When he was investigating the automobile industry (subordinate clause), Ralph Nader found that no American car was safe (main clause).

SS 5 • *Types of Sentences*

Clauses are the key to sentence classification.

a. *Simple sentences* have one independent clause and no subordinate clause. They may have many single-word or phrase modifiers, and both the subject and predicate may be compound.

> Both Sherwood Anderson and Edgar Lee Masters lived in the Middle West and wrote about life in the small towns there.

b. *Complex sentences* have one main clause and one or more subordinate clauses. More varied than simple sentences, complex sentences can be also more exact in showing relationships between elements. Subordination allows the writer to put his emphasis precisely where he wants it.

Inexact and unemphatic compound sentence:

> The corrected manuscript of *Brother to Dragons* was lost before publication and the published version is full of errors.

More exact and emphatic complex sentence:

> Because the corrected manuscript was lost before publication, the published version of *Brother to Dragons* is full of errors.

Inexact: Keats' *annus mirabilis* creatively was 1819, and he was seriously ill.

Better: Despite serious illness, Keats' *annus mirabilis* creatively was 1819.

Misplaced emphasis: Starbuck became increasingly alarmed at Ahab's erratic behavior; however, he could do nothing.

Better: Although Starbuck became increasingly alarmed at Ahab's erratic behavior, he could do nothing.

    c. *Compound sentences* are merely two or more simple sentences joined by coordinating conjunctions, colons, or semicolons (see SS 2c, Gr 1, and Gr 2).

> Poe mastered the technique of the short story, and he influenced later writers of the form.
>
> Poe distrusted the unaided intellect; consequently, he had Dupin solve mysteries by intuition and imagination as well as reason.

In a compound sentence the two main clauses should be of equal rank and importance, that is, coordinate. Excessive coordination can be monotonous, unemphatic, and inexact. Reduce the rank of less important material by subordination.

Excessive coordination: Rupert Brooke joined the navy, and he became ill, and he died quickly.

Better: After joining the navy, Rupert Brooke became fatally ill.

Excessive coordination: Emerson was interested in nature as a symbol of some transcendental truth, but Thoreau was concerned with its physical reality, and so Emerson was impatient with his friend's scientific exactness.

Improved: Emerson, interested in nature as a symbol of some transcendental truth, was impatient with the scientific exactness of his friend Thoreau, who was concerned with its physical reality.

Excessive coordination is often manifested in a long series of short, choppy, simple or compound sentences. (See *Sentence Variety*, pp. 12-14.)

    d. *Compound-complex* sentences have two or more main clauses and one or more subordinate clauses.

> Faust, who was dissatisfied with the terrible changefulness and uncertainty of life, yearned for completeness; therefore, he agreed to give his soul to Mephistopheles for the privilege of saying to the passing moment, "Oh stay, thou art so fair."

SS 6 • *Sentence Effectiveness*

Accuracy and clarity should be your first goals in composing sentences; economy and variety are next. Do not expect instant excellence: most good sentences are probably achieved by rewriting.

Repetition and wordiness confuse, bore, and irritate the reader. Repeat words only for emphasis and clarity. Carefully substitute pronouns to make your meaning clear.

Repetitious and wordy: I was delighted to receive a review copy of H. E. Bates' *The Four Beauties*. *The Four Beauties* is a delightful book, which I enjoyed reading. I am delighted to recommend it highly, and I think most readers will enjoy reading *The Four Beauties*.

Improved: I enjoyed reading H. E. Bates' *The Four Beauties*, and I recommend it highly.

Repetition of meaning (redundancy) can be avoided by thinking carefully about the meaning of each word you use. Note the redundancy of the following expressions.

this day and age	due to the fact that
the modern world of today	come in contact with
true facts	old and antiquated
usual rules	square in shape
promise for the future	a mile in length
the fall of the year	free gifts

Obtrusive repetition of sound may grate on the nerves. Alliteration, rhyme, and consonance that call attention to themselves rather than the ideas expressed should be reserved for poetry.

He proposed a prolonged period of probation.

I was relieved to see the leaves returning.

Seldom do birds sing when on the wing.

Sentence structure also should be varied. (See *Sentence Variety*, pp. 12-14.)

a. *Economy*. Deadwood, empty words and phrases that clutter sentences, should be pruned. Be wary if you find yourself writing phrases with words like *case, character, fact, field, line, manner, nature, type*. Such circumlocutions add nothing but length to sentences.

Wordy: His field of interest was in the nature of linguisitics.
Direct: He was interested in linguistics.

Wordy: The reason that Vonnegut wrote the book was for the purpose of expressing his outrage at man's inhumanity to man.
Direct: Vonnegut wrote the book to express his outrage at man's inhumanity to man.

Eliminate wordy phrases.

> by means of (by)
> in relation to (with)
> in connection with (with)
> of great importance (important)
> advance notice (notice)

Avoid overusing the passive voice, which often is impersonal, wordy, and indirect.

Weak: The biological bases of human behavior were called to the attention of Desmond Morris by the evidence from primate behavior.
Better: Desmond Morris saw primate behavior as evidence that human behavior has a biological basis.

Weak: *The Naked Ape* was written by him in this belief.
Better: He wrote *The Naked Ape* in this belief.

Eliminate unneeded *that's* and *which's.*

> The design [that] Chaucer intended for the tales was never realized.
> The California condor, [which is] one of our most spectacular birds, is nearing extinction.

Avoid *the use of.*

> He won by [the use of] fraud and chicanery.

When possible, let a verb rather than a noun convey your meaning.

Weak: Hitchcock's mysteries always have good plots.
Better: Hitchcock always plots his mysteries well.

Weak: The story was about a man in attendance at his own funeral.

Better: The story was about a man who attended his own funeral.

b. *Parallelism*. Parallelism, the process of putting equal sentence elements into similar grammatical constructions, gives sentences precision, balance, symmetry, coherence, and control. Balance words with words, phrases with phrases, clauses with clauses, sentences with sentences.

> "I wanted to live deep and suck out all the marrow of life, to live so sturdily and Spartan-like as to put to rout all that was not life, to cut a broad swath and shave close, to drive life into a corner, and to reduce it to its lowest terms. . . ."
>
> *Thoreau,* Walden

> "But in a larger sense, we cannot dedicate, we cannot consecrate, we cannot hallow this ground."
>
> *Lincoln, "The Gettysburg Address"*

You should usually repeat the paralleling connectives for clarity.

> Most critics admire *The Marble Faun for* the grandeur of its theme but not *for* its style.

Failure to make coordinate elements parallel causes a lack of exactness and clarity.

Inexact: At the University of Virginia, Faulkner spoke about his life, what he liked to read, and how he structured his novels.
Better: At the University of Virginia, Faulkner spoke about his life, his reading, and the structure of his novels.

Inexact: W. H. Auden is a distinguished poet, critic, and he also writes librettos.
Better: W. H. Auden is a distinguished poet, critic, and librettist.

Unbalanced: I read Virginia Woolf not for her polished style but because she is extremely subtle.
Balanced: I read Virginia Woolf not for her polished style but for her subtlety.

c. *Sentence Length, Variety, and Emphasis*. Excessively long sentences can confuse and daunt the reader, but several short ones can quicken his pace.

> "Delta Autumn," one of Faulkner's most significant and best known short stories, has as its theme the relationship of an individual to others and to the land, in other words, love and

conservation; and the main point seems to be that if one fails to love the land one will fail to love people, for Roth's killing the doe underscores his brutal treatment of his mistress. (This breathlessly long sentence should be divided into several shorter, more effective ones.)

On the other hand, a string of short, choppy sentences is monotonous and dull.

Hamlet is Shakespeare's most popular tragedy. It is about revenge and murder. This is a popular kind of plot. It has a great deal of action. There are fights and duels.

Improved: *Hamlet* is Shakespeare's most popular play, partly because its plot is concerned with revenge and murder, and partly because, with its fights and duels, it has an abundance of action.

Similarly, change pace and gain emphasis by varying the length of your sentences. Structure the sentence to emphasize what is most important.

Avoid monotony and gain emphasis and variety by varying the normal subject-verb-object word order. Frequent inversion, however, creates a pseudo-literary style.

The Nobel Prize Boris Pasternack refused. This refusal I could not understand.

Lonely are the brave.

Never would Beckett compromise with King Henry.

Avoid a long series of sentences that invariably begin with the subject.

Hawthorne, like Thoreau, dreamed of a simple country life of honest labor. He went to Brook Farm to pursue this goal. He was, however, disappointed. He found that he could not combine writing and physical labor. He then gave up the experiment.

Improved: Like Thoreau, Hawthorne dreamed of a simple country life of honest labor; but when he pursued his goal at Brook Farm, he found writing and physical work so incompatible that he disappointedly gave up the experiment.

Postponed subjects with *it* and *there*, though wordy, can occasionally be emphatic.

"There are more things in heaven and earth than are dreamt of in your philosophy." [Hamlet to Horatio.]

Achieve variety and emphasis by placing important words at the beginning or end of the sentence. Sentences should begin and end as strongly as possible.

Weak: However, Julian Huxley stated that there is no biological basis for war.
Improved: War, Julian Huxley maintained, has no biological basis.

Similarly, gain emphasis by using periodic sentences which hold the reader in suspense by keeping the main ideas until the end.

Unemphatic: Any story ends in death if continued long enough.
Better: Any story, if continued long enough, ends in death.

Occasionally use the passive voice for emphasis and variety. The passive can be used effectively if the agent is unknown (*Obviously a murder has been committed*), for forces of history (*By 1900 the frontier was tamed*), and to emphasize the receiver of the action (*Wilfred Owen was killed one week before the Armistice*).

Purposeful repetition can be a powerful way to gain emphasis.

> "We shall fight in France, we shall fight on the seas and oceans, we shall fight with growing confidence and growing strength in the air, we shall fight on the beaches, we shall fight on the landing grounds, we shall fight in the fields and in the streets, we shall fight in the hills."
>
> *Winston Churchill*

Balance effectively emphasizes contrasts.

> To err is human, to forgive divine.
>
> *Alexander Pope*

Vary sentence length for emphasis.

> Throughout his world travels and his many misfortunes Candide searched for his lovely, lost Cunegonde. Finally he found a miserable, shrewish, toothless hag. It was Cunegonde.

Note: Keep in mind that clarity and naturalness are greater virtues than emphasis and variety.

2

Paragraphs

Par

Words make up sentences, sentences make paragraphs, and paragraphs develop the theme. The writer thus constructs his theme out of paragraph units, groups of related sentences. The first line is usually indented to indicate a new unit of thought.

Classified according to their purpose, paragraphs are of several types: narrative, which tells a story; descriptive, which tells how something looks; expository, which explains something; and argumentative, which tries to convince. Most college writing courses are concerned primarily with the two latter kind.

The following paragraph is a description of Sherlock Holmes through the eyes of Dr. Watson:

> As the week went by, my interest in him and my curiosity as to his aims in life gradually deepened and increased. His very person and appearance were such as to strike the attention of the most casual observer. In height he was rather over six feet, and so excessively lean that he seemed to be considerably taller. His eyes were sharp and piercing, save during those intervals of torpor to which I have alluded; and his thin, hawk-like nose gave his whole expression an air of alertness and decision. His chin, too, had the prominence and squareness which mark the man of determination. His hands were invariably blotted with ink and stained with chemicals, yet he was possessed of extraordinary delicacy of touch, as I frequently had occasion to observe when I watched him manipulating his fragile philosophical instruments.
>
> *Sir Arthur Conan Doyle,* A Study in Scarlet

In this paragraph Guy Chapman narrates an incident from his experiences in World War I:

During that morning gallant pairs of stretcher bearers sometimes staggered through the storm with a groaning burden. The wounded were bound up, doped, and laid down, until the passage was filled with maimed and semi-conscious soldiers. None could be got away. The enemy guns concentrated on the line of the Bassevillebeek and the wood to prevent supports coming through. The shelling never ceased. The bursts at the edge of Dumbarton Lakes looked like woodmen's fires of autumn leaves. Glanville looked in for a moment, grinned and went back to his Stokes guns. The colonel led me over to the company of the 10th who were holding the gap between ourselves and the battalion on our right. Their tiny hovel was filled to the brim; one dodged in hastily hoping that nothing would push one forward from behind.

A Passionate Prodigality

In argumentative paragraphs the writer attempts to convince the reader of the correctness of his ideas.

There are valid reasons for saving wilderness. One is simply *noblesse oblige*: the conviction that priceless esthetic and scientific values are involved and that posterity will despise us for degrading them. Another is that the organization of biological communities is poorly understood. Ecologists therefore need samples of primitive landscapes for study, both to build up the basis of their science—to extend human knowledge—and to lay groundwork for management techniques.

Archie Carr, "Thoughts on Wilderness Preservation,"
Audubon, *September, 1969*

Expository paragraphs explain something.

Camp taste is, above all, a mode of enjoyment, of appreciation—not judgment. Camp is generous. It wants to enjoy. It only seems like malice, cynicism. (Or, if it is cynicism, it's not a ruthless but a sweet cynicism.) Camp taste doesn't propose that it is in bad taste to be serious; it doesn't sneer at someone who succeeds in being seriously dramatic. What it does is to find the success in certain passionate failures.

Susan Sontag, "Notes on 'Camp' "

The convention of writing in paragraphs aids both the writer and the reader. The writer in grouping related sentences to present one aspect of his thesis actually is writing a miniature theme with a single subject and tone. He can thus focus his attention and concentrate his energies on one part of his larger subject at a time. The division into paragraphs helps the reader by indicating the end of one part of the discussion and the beginning of another.

Par 1 • *Unity*

The effectiveness of good paragraphs depends largely upon their having unity; that is, they must have one subject and one tone. In concentrating on one specific topic you should include only details that develop this topic, no matter how enchanting and interesting side issues may appear. And you should have enough information about the paragraph topic for completeness. Your tone, or attitude toward the subject, should also remain consistent throughout the paragraph. A hodgepodge of sentences, some humorous or ironical, others serious and direct, merely puzzles the reader.

The foundation for a unified paragraph is a strong topic sentence—the sentence that gives the key idea, the central thought or purpose of the paragraph. The topic sentence is the generative sentence, indicating that more will be said. For clarity the topic sentence should usually be placed at or near the beginning of the paragraph. Digressive paragraphs and ones without strong topic sentences make excessive demands on the reader, and they hinder communication—always the main consideration. Notice how the following paragraph is a clear, self-contained unit.

> It is hardly news that in best-sellerdom we frequently wind up with the hero coming to terms and settling down in Scarsdale, or wherever, knowing himself. And on Broadway, in the third act, someone says, "Look, why don't you just love each other?" and the protagonist, throwing his hand to his forehead, cries, "Oh God, why didn't *I* think of that!" and before the bulldozing action of love, all else collapses—verisimilitude, truth, and interest. It is like "Dover Beach" ending happily for Matthew Arnold, and for us, because the poet is standing at the window with a woman who understands him. If the investigation of our times and the impact of these times upon human personality were to become the sole property of Wouk, Weidman, Sloan Wilson, Cameron Hawley, and the theatrical amor-vincit-omnia boys it would indeed be unfortunate, for it would be somewhat like leaving sex to the pornographers, where again there is more to what is happening than first meets the eye.
>
> *Philip Roth, "Writing American Fiction"*

Par 2 • *Coherence*

The sentences of good paragraphs fit together into a connected whole. Paragraphs in which the sentences are closely related to one another so that the thought movement is orderly and never abrupt have coherence. Such paragraphs have no gaps in thought, no confusing leaps. Several devices can be used to tie a paragraph together:

1. Transitional connective words and phrases like *and, but, moreover, therefore, nevertheless, thus, for example*. (Avoid excessive use of such words, for they call attention to themselves so that the reader hears the machinery creak.)
2. Repetition of key words.
3. The use of pronouns.
4. Related sentence patterns.
5. By far the most important—logic: a clear, orderly progression from one point to the next in order to achieve continuity of thought.

The whole theme should also have coherence. The topic sentence of each paragraph should relate its paragraph to the central idea of the theme. In longer themes short transitional paragraphs may be useful to sum up what has been done, to introduce the new topic, or to show the relation between what has been done and what is to be done. But in themes of 350 to 1000 words such paragraphs are rarely needed.

Par 3 • *Length and Variety*

A paragraph should be long enough to develop and convey an idea fully but not long enough to alienate the reader. In general, increase paragraph lengths with the complexity of the material. Overuse of short paragraphs jerks both the eyes and the mind about uncomfortably. Paragraphs of only one or two sentences appear superficial; such short paragraphs, which are usually mere fragments of ideas, may be expanded with evidence, illustration, or explanation, or combined with other short paragraphs, or perhaps omitted entirely.

To avoid monotony within the paragraph, vary the type and length of the sentences. To avoid monotony in longer themes, vary paragraph length for emphasis. Notice the effective use of sentence variety as well as the appropriate length of the illustrative paragraphs in Par 4.

Par 4 • *Methods of Organization*

Paragraphs may be developed in the following basic ways:

a. *Exemplification*:

1. The use of several or many facts, examples, details, or reasons to support the topic sentence of the paragraph.
2. The use of one detailed example to clarify or to prove a generalization.

A spurning of our world—though of a much different order—seems to occur in another of our most talented writers, Bernard Malamud. Even, one recalls, when Malamud writes a book about baseball, a book called *The Natural*, it is not baseball as it is played in Yankee Stadium, but a wild, wacky baseball, where a player who is instructed to knock the cover off the ball promptly steps up to the plate and knocks it off; the batter swings and the inner hard string core of the ball goes looping out to centerfield, where the confused fielder commences to tangle himself in the unwinding sphere; then the shortstop runs out, and with his teeth, bites the centerfielder and the ball free from one another. Though *The Natural* is not Malamud's most successful, nor his most significant book, it is at any rate our introduction to his world, which has a kind of historical relationship to our own, but is by no means a replica of it. By historical I mean that there are really things called baseball players and really things called Jews, but there much of the similarity ends. The Jews of *The Magic Barrel* and the Jews of *The Assistant*, I have reason to suspect, are not the Jews of New York City or Chicago. They are a kind of invention, a metaphor to stand for certain human possibilities and certain human promises, and I find myself further inclined to believe this when I read of a statement attributed to Malamud which goes, "All men are Jews." In fact we know this is not so; even the men who are Jews aren't sure they're Jews. But Malamud, as a writer of fiction, has not shown specific interest in the anxieties and dilemmas and corruptions of the modern American Jew, the Jew we think of as characteristic of our times; rather, his people live in a timeless depression and a placeless Lower East Side; their society is not affluent, their predicaments not cultural. I am not saying—one cannot, of Malamud—that he has spurned life or an examination of the difficulties of being human. What it is to be human, to be humane, is his subject; connection, indebtedness, responsibility, these are his moral concerns. What I do mean to point out is that he does not—or has not yet—found the contemporary scene a proper or sufficient backdrop for his tales of heartlessness and heartache, of suffering and regeneration.

Philip Roth, "Writing American Fiction"

b. *Comparison and contrast*: the enumeration of similarities or differences between two or more subjects. The writer classifies, explains, or analyzes one thing by holding it up against another. The subjects may be dealt with alternately or in sequence. The latter method, in which one topic is treated fully and then the other, is the easier one to handle. With either method you should set up a clear basis for comparison in order to be consistent and logical.

In the final instance tragedy is an appraisal of human fate, a measure of the absolute. The grotesque is a critisicm of the absolute in the name of frail human experience. That is why tragedy brings catharsis, while grotesque offers no consolation whatsoever. "Tragedy," wrote Gorgias of Leontium, "is a swindle in which the swindler is more just that the swindled, and the swindled wiser than the swindler." One may travesty this aphorism by saying that grotesque is a swindle in which the swindled is more just than the swindler, and the swindler wiser than the swindled. Clare Zachanassian in Durrenmatt's *Visit* is wiser than Anton Schill, but he is more just than she is. Schill's death, like Polonius's death in *Hamlet*, is grotesque. Neither Schill nor the inhabitants of Gullen are tragic heroes. The old lady with her artificial breasts, teeth and limbs is not a goddess; she hardly even exists, she might almost have been invented. Schill and the people of Gullen find themselves in a situation in which there is no room for tragedy, but only for grotesque. "Comedy," writes Ionesco in his *Experience du theatre*, "is a feeling of absurdity, and seems more hopeless than tragedy; comedy allows no way out of a given situation."

Jon Kott, "King Lear or Endgame"

c. *Definition*: the explanation of what a thing is by first relating it to similar things of the same class and then differentiating it from other members of that class. The two basic steps, then, are classification and differentiation. An extended definition for a paragraph or a theme can dwell upon either the class or the differentiae.

They say it is a critic's phrase, Black Humor, and that whatever it is, you can count on it to fizzle after a bit. And besides, don't these fellows just write about outcasts? Fags, junkies, hunchbacks, "preverts," Negroes, Jews, other assorted losers? What's that got to do with anything anyway? I think they may be wrong on that first count. I have a hunch Black Humor has probably always been around, always will be around, under some name or other, as long as there are disguises to be peeled back, as long as there are thoughts no one else cares to think. And as to the idea that these writers do not deal with "representative" types—it may be that you can govern by consensus. And it may be that if you are doing anything as high-minded as examining society, the very best way to go about it is by examining first its throwaways, the ones who can't or won't keep in step (in step with what?). And who knows? Perhaps "bad" behavior of a certain kind is better than "good" behavior. The American Health Society claims that only 5% of syphilis is spread by prostitutes.

Bruce Jay Friedman, "Black Humor"

d. *Cause and effect*: explanation by moving deductively from cause to effect or inductively from effect to cause. Keep in mind the complexity of causation—most effects have a multiplicity of causes. (See Log h.)

To take one trivial fact, the ready-made clothing industry was an offshoot of the mass production of blue uniforms—and would not this standardization of fashion, after the sartorial whim, confusion, fantasy and individualism of an earlier time, have some effect on man's relation to man? But to leap from the trivial to the grand, the War prepared the way for the winning of the West. Before the War a transcontinental railroad was already being planned, and execution was being delayed primarily by debate about the route to take, a debate which in itself sprang from, and contributed something to, the intersectional acrimony. After the War, debate did not long delay action. But the War did more than remove impediment to this scheme. It released enormous energies, new drives and know-how for the sudden and massive occupation of the continent. And for the great adventure there was a new cutting edge of profit.

Robert Penn Warren, The Legacy of the Civil War

e. *Analogy*: a use of the familiar to explain the unfamiliar; frequently an effective method to make abstract and difficult subjects more tangible and vivid. Do not try the reader's patience by using an analogy to explain the obvious. (See Log o.)

We may illustrate the course which thought has hitherto run by likening it to a web woven of three different threads—the black thread of magic, the red thread of religion, and the white thread of science, if under science we may include those simple truths, drawn from observation of nature, of which men in all ages have possessed a store. Could we then survey the web of thought from the beginning, we should probably perceive it to be at first a chequer of black and white, a patchwork of true and false notions, hardly tinged as yet by the red thread of religion. But carry your eye farther along the fabric and you will remark that, while the black and white chequer still runs through it, there rests on the middle portion of the web, where religion has entered most deeply into its texture, a dark crimson stain, which shades off insensibly into a lighter tint as the white thread of science is woven more and more into the tissue. To a web thus chequered and stained, thus shot with threads of diverse hues, but gradually changing colour the farther it is unrolled, the state of modern thought, with all its divergent aims and conflicting tendencies, may be compared. Will the great movement which for centuries has been slowly altering the complexion of thought be continued in the near future? Or will a reaction set in which may arrest progress and even undo much that has been done? To keep up our parable, what will be the colour of the web which the Fates are now weaving on the humming loom of time? Will it be white or red? We cannot tell. A faint glimmering light illumines the backward portion of the web. Clouds and thick darkness hide the other end.

Sir James G. Frazer, "Myth in Primitive Thought"

f. *Analysis*: explanation by reducing the topic to its component parts.

> And what about me? What kind of feelings do I have about Negroes today? What happened to me, from Brooklyn, who grew up fearing and envying and hating Negroes? Now that Brooklyn is behind me, do I fear them and envy them and hate them still? The answer is yes, but not in the same proportions and certainly not in the same way. I now live on the upper west side of Manhattan, where there are many Negroes and many Puerto Ricans, and there are nights when I experience the old apprehensiveness again, and there are streets that I avoid when I am walking in the dark, as there were streets that I avoided when I was a child. I find that I am not afraid of Puerto Ricans, but I cannot restrain my nervousness whenever I pass a group of Negroes standing in front of a bar or sauntering down the street. I know now, as I did not know when I was a child, that power is on my side, that the police are working for me and not for them. And knowing this I feel ashamed and guilty, like the good liberal I have grown up to be. Yet the twinges of fear and the resentment they bring and the self-contempt they arouse are not to be gainsaid.

> *Norman Podhoretz, "My Negro Problem—and Ours"*

g. *Classification*: putting the parts of a subject into classes in which the members have significant elements in common.

> Greek mythology is largely made up of stories about gods and goddesses, but it must not be read as a kind of Greek Bible, an account of the Greek religion. According to the most modern idea, a real myth has nothing to do with religion. It is an explanation of something in nature; how, for instance, any and everything in the universe came into existence; men, animals, this or that tree or flower, the sun, the moon, the stars, storms, eruptions, earthquakes, all that is and all that happens. Thunder and lightning are caused when Zeus hurls his thunderbolt. A volcano erupts because a terrible creature is imprisoned in the mountain and every now and then struggles to get free. The Dipper, the constellation, called also the Great Bear, does not set below the horizon because a goddess once was angry at it and decreed that it should never sink into the sea. Myths are early science, the result of men's first trying to explain what they saw around them. But there are many so-called myths which explain nothing at all. These tales are pure entertainment, the sort of thing people would tell each other on a long winter's evening. The story of Pygmalion and Galatea is an example; it has no conceivable connection with any event in nature. Neither has the Quest of the Golden Fleece, nor Orpheus and Eurydice, nor many another. This fact is now generally accepted; and we do not have to try to find in every mythological heroine the moon or the dawn and

in every hero's life a sun myth. The stories are early literature as well
as early science.

Edith Hamilton, Mythology

Par 5 • *Introductory and Concluding Paragraphs*

Introductory paragraphs. Most themes benefit by having a separate
paragraph devoted to orienting and interesting the reader. This paragraph should,
first, inform the reader clearly and succinctly of the theme's purpose and scope.
Second, it should, if possible, gain his attention and interest.

Concluding paragraphs. The final impression is usually the lasting one; hence,
the last paragraph is the most emphatic one in your theme. Here you should
indicate to the reader that you have finished what you set out to do. Too many
beginning writers leave the impression that they just quit arbitrarily. Long papers
usually require as a conclusion a full paragraph summary; short themes rarely do;
but you should end on a strong point—one you want the reader to remember.

The following introductory and concluding paragraphs by Konrad Lorenz
illustrate several techniques for effectively beginning and ending a paper. In the
introduction he explains the problem he deals with in the essay, and in the
conclusion he explains what can be done about it, thus ending strongly on his
main point.

In reality, militant enthusiasm is a specialized form of communal
aggression, clearly distinct from any yet functionally related to the
more primitive forms of petty individual aggression. Every man of
normally strong emotions knows, from his own experience, the
subjective phenomena that go hand in hand with the response of
militant enthusiasm. A shiver runs down the back and, as more exact
observation shows, along the outside of both arms. One soars elated,
above all the ties of everyday life, one is ready to abandon all for the
call of what, in the moment of this specific emotion, seems to be
sacred duty. All obstacles in its path become unimportant; the
instinctive inhibitions against hurting or killing one's fellows lose,
unfortunately, much of their power. Rational considerations,
criticism, and all reasonable arguments against the behavior dictated
by militant enthusiasm are silenced by an amazing reversal of all
values, making them appear not only untenable but base and
dishonorable. Men may enjoy the feeling of absolute righteousness
even while they commit atrocities. Conceptual thought and moral
responsibility are at their lowest ebb. As a Ukrainian proverb says:
"When the banner is unfurled, all reason is in the trumpet."

. . .

In other words, the need to control, by wise rational responsibility, all our emotional allegiances to cultural values is as great as,

if not greater than, the necessity to keep in check our other instincts. None of them can ever have such devastating effects as unbridled militant enthusiasm when it infects and overrides all other considerations by its single-mindedness and its specious nobility. It is not enthusiasm in itself that is in any way noble, but humanity's great goals which it can be called upon to defend. That indeed is the Janus head of man: The only being capable of dedicating himself to the very highest moral and ethical values requires for this purpose a phylogenetically adapted mechanism of behavior whose animal properties bring with them the danger that he kill his brother, convinced that he is doing so in the interests of these very same high values. *Ecce homo*!

Konrad Lorenz, "Ecce Homo"

3

Grammar

Gr

Gr 1 • *Comma Splice or Comma Fault* (CS)

Two independent clauses require punctuation more forceful than a comma unless the clauses are linked by a coordinate conjunction. Even conjunctive abverbs like *thus, however, therefore, consequently, moreover, otherwise, meanwhile,* and *then* need a mark stronger than a comma. These conjunctive adverbs are weaker connectives than coordinate conjunctions. Many teachers still regard the comma splice, two independent clauses joined by only a comma, as a heinous offense, revealing ignorance of sentence structure. So be cautious even when, occasionally, a comma fault may seem to serve your purpose better than conventional punctuation.

> There is nothing really new about the material comfort of our civilization, men could have installed bathrooms, central heating, and sanitary plumbing any time during the last three or four thousand years. (Here the comma fault causes no misunderstanding.)

Comma faults are especially troublesome to the reader when a modifying phrase or clause comes between the two independent clauses so that he cannot determine to which the modifier belongs.

> Robert Lowell's experiments in drama have been successful, I think, his adaptation of Melville's *Benito Cereno* was a popular play.

Correct comma faults in one of three ways: add a coordinating conjunction, subordinate one of the clauses, or separate the two clauses with a semicolon or a period.

25

Comma fault:

The Homecoming is a difficult play, it mystifies the audience.

Correction:

1. *The Homecoming* is a difficult play, and it mystifies the audience. (Add the coordinating conjunction *and*.)
2. Because *The Homecoming* is a difficult play, it mystifies the audience. (Subordinate the first clause to the second.)
3. *The Homecoming* is a difficult play; it mystifies the audience. (Replace the comma with the stronger semicolon.)

Note: Many writers feel that comma faults are justified in sentences made up of three or more parallel clauses, especially if the clauses are closely related in thought and structure and present no danger of misreading.

They ran through the briars, they ran through the brambles, they ran through the bushes where a rabbit couldn't go.

Gr 2 • *Fused or Run-On Sentence* (FS)

A run-on sentence is merely a comma fault without the comma or other punctuation: independent clauses are run together without a coordinating conjunction. The clauses should be separated by a semicolon or a period.

The Homecoming is a difficult play it mystifies the audience.

Because they are a radical departure from convention, fused sentences call attention to themselves and cast doubt on the writer's literacy. There is little or no reason for run-on sentences other than carelessness. They are corrected in the same ways as comma faults.

Gr 3 • *Sentence Fragment* (Frag)

A sentence fragment is usually less than a complete thought. It lacks a subject or complete verb. Although fragments are common in creative and informal writing, they should be avoided in formal composition. The following are fragments and some ways to correct them.

Fragment: Wolfe's *Look Homeward, Angel* was his first novel. Perhaps his best.

Corrected: Wolfe's *Look Homeward, Angel* was his first and, perhaps, best novel.

Join a subordinate clause to the main sentence.

Fragment: I admire Pound's *Cantos*. Although I find his politics deplorable.
Corrected: Although I find Pound's politics deplorable, I admire his *Cantos*.

Turn a dependent clause into an independent clause.

Fragment: Tennyson's "The Charge of the Light Brigade" seems jingoistic and melodramatic. Although some critics defend it.
Corrected: Tennyson's "The Charge of the Light Brigade" seems jingoistic and melodramatic. Some critics, however, defend it.

Complete a short-circuited or incomplete thought.

Fragment: *Candide* is a radical book. No possible hope and work only an anodyne.
Corrected: *Candide* is a radical book, because in it Voltaire indicates that no hope is possible and that work is only an anodyne.

Join a fragmented afterthought to the main sentence, usually with a dash or colon.

Fragment: Robert Stone's *Hall of Mirrors* develops the theme that in today's world survival is immoral. A deeply disturbing idea.
Corrected: Robert Stone's *Hall of Mirrors* develops the theme that in today's world survival is immoral—a deeply disturbing idea.

Fragment: Three recent American novelists have won the Nobel Prize. Hemingway, Faulkner, and Steinbeck.
Corrected: Three recent American novelists have won the Nobel Prize: Hemingway, Faulkner, and Steinbeck.

Most of the time fragments are logically as well as grammatically incomplete. But they can be useful in the following ways.

a. Dialogue (conversation fragments are usual):

"Where are you going?"
"Home."

b. Answers to questions:

What has O'Neill's experimentation in stage techniques contributed to modern drama? Little or nothing.

c. Common transitional expressions:

Now for a look at innovations in stage design.

d. Descriptions:

Yes, and of the rank slow river, and of tomatoes rotten on the vine; the smell of rain wet plums and boiling quinces; of rotten lily-pads; and of foul weeds rotting in green marsh scum; and of the exquisite sme.: of the South, clean but funky like a big woman; of soaking trees and the earth after heavy rain. (Verbs are simply not needed in this description from Thomas Wolfe's *Look Homeward, Angel*.)

e. Narrative passages suggesting disconnected thought or stream of consciousness:

William Styron's portrayal of the dying thoughts of a disturbed girl in *Lie Down in Darkness* uses the confusion of sentence fragments to suggest mental derangement: "I say, oh pooh. Oh pooh. Must be proper. Oh most proper. Powerful. Oh most powerful. Oh must."

Gr 4 • *Agreement of Subject and Verb* (Agr)

A verb should agree with its subject in person and number.

The shadow knows.
Rod McKuen and Lawrence Cohen know what kind of poetry sells.

In English all verbs except *to be* have only two forms (singular and plural) in the present tense and only one form in the past tense; but despite this simplicity, several constructions are especially troublesome.

a. The verb agrees with the subject, not with the predicate noun.

As a young man Benjamin Franklin's chief concern was books.

b. With expletives (*there is* and *there are* sentences) the subject comes after the verb and determines its number.

"There are more *things* in heaven and earth than are dreamt of in your philosophy."
In an Albee play there is no *way* to know for certain any final meanings.

The expletive *it* always takes a singular verb.

> It is ensemble playing and a varied repertoire which make the Royal Shakespeare Company so successful.

c. In sentences like "Voltaire was one of those eighteenth-century satirists who were fierce haters" the subject (*who*) of the dependent clause agrees with the nearest antecedent (*satirists*) and, thus, usually requires a plural verb (in this sentence, *were*).

> Picasso's *Guernica* is one of those paintings that have profound political implications. (The subject of *have* is *that*; the antecedent of *that* is paintings; therefore, *that* is plural and takes a plural verb.)

d. When *or, nor, either ... or, neither ... nor* join subjects, sometimes a singular verb is required, sometimes a plural one. If the subjects are singular and regarded as separate, the verb is singular.

> Concerning the choices offered characters in melodramas, one alternative or the other *is* not disastrous.

If both subjects are plural or if both are singular but not regarded as separate, a plural verb is required.

> No tragic problems or dilemmas *are* dramatized in melodramas.

e. If one subject is plural and the other singular, usually the verb agrees with the nearer subject.

> Neither the Italian directors nor Godard *permits* studio intervention.

f. The number of a subject is not altered by attaching another noun to it by such expressions as *with, along with*, or *in addition to*.

> This critic along with the reading public *judges Herzog* to be a successful novel.

g. Collective nouns (team, committee, faculty) require singular verbs when the group is a unit.

> At most movies the audience *is* unsophisticated.

But if the collective noun refers to the individuals of the group, a plural noun is needed.

> The awards committee *do* not *agree* among themselves.

h. Measurements and figures need singular verbs if the amount is considered as a unit.

Fifteen dollars *is* too much to spend on a Broadway play.

But if the amount is regarded as individual units, a plural verb should be used.

At least three *have donated* their awards to charity.

i. Indefinite pronouns such as *each, either, neither, anyone, anything, someone, one, everyone, nobody* take singular verbs.

Nobody knows the troubles I've seen.
Everyone has experienced the emotions evoked in Gray's "Elegy."

j. When nouns like *type* and *part* are used before a phrase with plural nouns, singular verbs are required.

The best part of Ross McDonald's mysteries *is* the whines of self-pity of the villains when they are caught.

k. Nouns that are plural in form but singular in meaning usually take singular verbs.

Aesthetics *is* not a precise science.

But since some words like *environs* take plural verbs, one should consult a dictionary in all doubtful cases.

l. Titles and words referred to as words take singular verbs.

Lack's *Darwin's Finches documents* the adaptive radiation that led to Darwin's discoveries.
"Kids" *is* colloquial.

Gr 5 • *Agreement of Pronoun and Antecedent* (**Agr**)

Pronouns agree with their antecedents (the words to which they refer) in person, number, and gender.

Gilbert and Sullivan collaborated on *their* comic operas.
Wallace Stevens wrote *his* poems while working as an insurance executive.

Special Problems

a. Indefinite pronouns (such as *one, anyone, someone, everyone, each, either, neither*) are singular and so in formal usage pronouns referring to them are singular.

Everyone should accept *his* responsibility for population control.

b. Alternative subjects if singular connected by *or* or *nor* are singular and require a singular pronoun. If the alternative subjects are plural they require plural pronouns. If one is singular and the other plural the pronoun agrees with the nearer antecedent.

Neither Ibsen nor Shaw would alter *his* plays to gain public acceptance.

Either the critics or the author would have to revise *his* stand.

Either the author or the critics would have to revise *their* stand.

c. Collective nouns require singular or plural pronouns depending on whether the noun refers to the group as a whole or the individuals of the group.

The research committee voted unanimously to give *its* endorsement to his study of ethnology.

Rarely can a college faculty agree among *themselves*.

Gr 6 • *Pronoun Reference* (Ref)

Since a pronoun is a substitute for a noun, the noun it refers to should be readily apparent to avoid ambiguity.

a. Sometimes it is best to repeat the appropriate noun when the pronoun could refer to more than one antecedent.

Robert Frost was influential in obtaining Ezra Pound's release from prison; *he* had been sympathetic to the fascists. (Correct this ambiguous *he* by repeating *Pound*.)

b. *They* preceded by two plural nouns is often ambiguous. Make one of the nouns singular.

Ambiguous: Poets do not like to explain *their* meaning to *their* readers. *They* are naturally impatient with *their* obtuseness.

Clear: A poet does not like to explain *his* meaning to *his* readers. *He* is naturally impatient with *their* obtuseness.

c. For clarity, do not use pronouns to refer to ideas.

Unclear: I said that I was the first to understand Hopkins' real meaning, but the others did not believe *it*.

Clear: I said that I was the first to understand Hopkins' real meaning, but the others thought Bridges had been first.

Also avoid use of the vague *this*.

Vague: Hobbes wrote that life is "solitary, poor, nasty, mean, brutish, and short." *This* is quite pessimistic.

Clear: *This description* is quite pessimistic.

d. To keep from confusing the reader, avoid implied antecedents.

Confusing: When he was awarded the Bollingen Prize, *they* said that it was for his entire poetic output.

Clear: When he was awarded the Bollingen Prize, the committee said that it was for his entire poetic output.

e. Use *who* to refer to persons, *which* to things, *that* to either.

Edmund Blunden was the poet *who* (or *that*, but not *which*) held the Chair of Poetry at Oxford.

Gr 7 • *Case* (Case)

Modern English retains only three case inflections—nominative (subject forms), possessive, and objective (object forms). Nouns inflect only for the possessive case. Personal pronouns—*I, he, she, we, they*—and the relative pronoun *who* change form for all three of the cases.

Nominative (subject) case	Possessive case	Objective (object) case
I	my (mine)	me
he	his	him
she	her (hers)	her
we	our (ours)	us
they	their (theirs)	them
who	whose	whom

Reflexive pronouns, used to indicate that the object is identical with the subject or to emphasize a noun, also are inflected.

> Virginia Woolf drowned *herself*.
> The author *himself* should read proof.

Avoid using "myself" as a substitute for "me." (I take only courses relevant to myself.)

a. The *nominative* case indicates that a pronoun is the subject of a sentence or is a predicate pronoun.

Subject: *She* is just a poor scullery maid.
Predicate noun: The queen shall be *she* who can wear this slipper.

If an entire clause is used as an object of a verb or preposition, the case of a pronoun is determined by its use in the clause.

> Once colleges accepted *whoever* applied. (*Whoever* functions as the subject of *applied*; the clause *whoever applied* is the object of *accepted*.)

Do not be confused by intervening phrases like *you know* or *I believe.*

> If Jeanne Moreau will not accept the role, *who* do you think will play the part? (*Who*, the relative pronoun, is in the nominative case since it is the subject of *will play*.)

b. The *objective* case is used for:

1. Direct objects. (Send *whomever* you want.)
2. Objects of prepositions. (He did not realize to *whom* he was speaking.)
3. Indirect objects. (Tell *him* the problem, not *me*.)
4. Objects of verbals. (Understanding *him* was always difficult.)
5. Subjects of infinitives. (I asked *him* to explain.)

c. The *possessive* case is used to show the relationship between:

1. Two nouns or a noun and a pronoun (Van Gogh's ear, his manuscript, *A Hard Day's Night*).
2. A noun or pronoun and a gerund. (Some were highly critical of James's leaving America.)

To form the possessive of nouns:

1. Add an apostrophe and an *s* for nouns not ending in *s*.
2. Add only an apostrophe for nouns ending in *s* (boys, the boys' game).
3. Add an apostrophe and an *s* if the additional *s* is pronounced; if not pronounced add only the apostrophe. (Thomas—Thomas's, Williams—Williams').

Do not use an apostrophe in forming the possessive of personal and relative pronouns (*his, theirs, whose*).

d. Problems involving case:

1. Pronouns in apposition are in the same case as the nouns they go with.

We workers must unite. (*We* is in the nominative case since it refers to *workers*, the subject.)
TV taught *us* viewers the dangers of mediocrity. (*Us* is in the objective case since it refers to viewers, the indirect object.)

2. Determine the case of a pronoun in an elliptical clause by finding its function in the clause if the clause were complete.

Hedda was far more determined than he. (Completed, the sentence would end: . . . than he was determined.)
Byron admired Satan more than Him. (". . . more than he admired Him.")

3. *Who* (nominative) and *whom* (objective) are sometimes confusing, partly because *who* is increasingly replacing *whom* in speech. In most writing a wrongly used *who* seems too colloquial and a wrongly used *whom* too pretentious or ignorant. Such sentences as "Who did you send the book to?" are acceptable in colloquial usage.
4. Similarly, written English generally requires the nominative case after the verb *to be*, although in colloquial usage the objective case is permissible.

It was he who made the discovery.
It's me.

Gr 8 • *Shifts* (Shifts)

Avoid shifts which result in awkwardness, inconsistency, or obscurity.

a. *Shift in number* (see also Gr 4, *Agreement of Subject and Verb*). For correctness and coherence avoid confusing shifts in number.

Inconsistent: The *CIA* has received much criticism. *Their* activities have been closely scrutinized.

Improved: The *CIA* has received much criticism. *Its* activities have been closely scrutinized.

Awkward: When *one* has read Kant thoroughly, *you* can begin to read Hegel.

Improved: When *one* has read Kant thoroughly, *he* can begin to read Hegel.

Improved: When *you* have read Kant thoroughly, *you* can begin to read Hegel.

b. *Shift in voice and subject*. Avoid confusing shifts between the active and passive voice. The resulting change in subjects causes inconsistency. The active voice should be maintained when the subject remains the active element.

Hawthorne soon realized the impossibility of combining manual labor and creative work; his participation in Brook Farm was set aside. ("He set aside his participation in Brook Farm" is better.)

Wilfred Owen returned to the front where his best poems were written. (". . . where he wrote his best poems" involves no shift in voice or subject.)

Audubon next journeyed to the South, but at first the bird life disappointed him. (The needless change in focus from Audubon to bird life can be avoided by writing instead ". . . but at first he was disappointed in the bird life.")

c. *Shift in tense*. Use the proper tenses of verbs to show how events are related in time.

1. Avoid indiscriminate shifts from past to present tense.

In the first act the chorus mourned the woes that had befallen Thebes. Suddenly Oedipus appears and they prostrated themselves at his feet. (Change *appears* to *appeared*.)

2. Indicate when two events occurred at different times in the past by keeping the sequence of tenses clear and consistent.

The spy in *The Spy Whom Came in from the Cold* agreed to the action, unaware that the officials already *planned* to sacrifice the girl. (The tense in the last clause should be past perfect *had planned* since the plans were complete before the agreement.)

The present perfect (with *has* or *have*) indicates recent past action or action begun in the past and continuing in the present; the past perfect (with *had*) indicates action that occurred in the more distant past.

3. Distinguish between direct and indirect discourse by adjusting the sequence of tenses.

Sartre said, "I refuse to accept the Nobel Prize."
Sartre said that he refused the Nobel Prize.
Sartre said, "I refused the Nobel Prize."
Sartre said that he had refused the Nobel Prize.

d. *Shift in mood*. Maintain consistency in mood by distinguishing between factual reference to a possibility and conditional reference which makes the same possibility less certain.

Inconsistent: If baseball players accept the reserve clause uncritically, they would be foolish.
Factual: If baseball players accept the reserve clause uncritically, they will be foolish.
Conditional: If baseball players accepted the reserve clause uncritically, they would be foolish.

The imperative mood—the command or request form of verbs—is used mainly in directions and exhortations. "Use only fresh limes." "Remember the Maine!" Use these forms carefully and infrequently in most themes.

Lawmakers must consider the overwhelming problem of urban blight. Quit dawdling and take direct action! ("They should quit dawdling and take direct action" loses little in emphasis and gains in clarity.)

The subjunctive mood, which is disappearing from informal speech, is used in some clauses that are concerned with possibilities instead of actualities. It is formed by using the singular of the verb *to be* and the plural form of the verb with a singular subject as in the following examples:

1. The subjunctive may be used in stating conditions that are false, impossible, or unlikely.

If I *were* in your shoes, I would accept the nomination.
Shaw wrote as if he *were* the only wise man.
To the uninformed writing good poetry seems as if it *were* easy.

2. The subjunctive may be used to indicate desirability and necessity.

I wish I *were* an apple on a tree.

Scrooge insisted that Bob Cratchit *work* on Christmas Eve.

He insisted that each player *be* in condition.

    3. The subjunctive may be used for commands, requests, or suggestions.

He demands that each student *come* to class and he asks that he *be* on time.

I strongly advise that he *borrow* no more money.

    e. *Shift in person*. Avoid awkward and inconsistent shifts in person.

Inconsistent: One should determine the author's purpose, and then you should analyze the way he achieves it.

Awkward: *He* said *he* hated to retire because people will always think of *you* as a quitter.

Note: In most expository writing one should use the first person infrequently. The first person plural (the editorial *we*) usually seems stilted.

    To refer directly to the reader, one can occasionally use the second person. But using *you* as an equivalent for *one* or *a person* sounds too informal and can be confusing.

Gr 9 • *Dangling Construction* (Dgl)

    A modifying phrase dangles if it has nothing in the sentence to modify or if it appears to modify an inappropriate word. A dangling phrase can make a sentence ludicrous and confusing.

    a. Dangling participial phrases can be corrected by (1) adding a noun or pronoun to which the phrase can logically refer or (2) making the participial phrase into a dependent clause.

Dangling: Being from the country, Dr. Johnson's hatred of rural life irritated me.

Clearer: Being from the country, I was irritated by Dr. Johnson's hatred of rural life.

Clearer: Because I am from the country, Dr. Johnson's hatred of rural life irritated me.

Dangling: Driving through the Everglades, the drought-stricken landscape was oppressive.

Clearer: Driving through the Everglades, I found the drought-stricken landscape oppressive.

Clearer: While I was driving through the Everglades, the drought-stricken landscape was oppressive.

   b. A dangling gerund, which has no noun or pronoun to perform the described action, can be remedied by naming the actor.

Dangling: By requiring manufacturers to clean up their wastes, the rivers would slowly become pure again.

Clearer: By requiring manufacturers to clear up their wastes, we could slowly make our rivers pure again.

   c. Dangling elliptical clauses and phrases, which have an implied subject or verb, can be unclear unless the implied subject is identical with the subject of the main clause. Supply a subject to prevent misreading.

Dangling: When only ten years old Hemingway's father allowed him to watch a Caesarean delivery.

Clearer: When Hemingway was only ten years old, his father allowed him to watch a Caesarean delivery.

   d. Dangling infinitive phrases can be corrected by specifying the performer of the action.

Dangling: To write knowledgeably about any novel, the secondary sources must be consulted.

Clearer: To write knowledgeably about any novel, the critic must consult the secondary sources.

Gr 10 • *Squinting Constructions* (Sq)

   Squinting constructions—modifiers that can logically refer to either a preceding or a following word—cause misreading.

   The National Football League agreed readily to accept the new franchises. (The adverb *readily* could modify the verb *agreed* or the infinitive *to accept*.)

   They announced last August they had decided. (Did they make the announcement last August or did they decide then?)

Gr 11 • *Misplaced Modifiers* (Mm)

Modifiers and the words they modify should be as close together as possible.

a. Adverbs

Misplaced: On first reading, many of Wallace Stevens' poems hardly make any sense.

Improved: On first reading, many of Wallace Stevens' poems make hardly any sense.

Misplaced: I only understood "Thirteen Ways of Looking at a Blackbird" after several readings.

Improved: I understood "Thirteen Ways of Looking at a Blackbird" only after several readings.

b. Prepositional phrases

1. Adjectival prepositional phrases immediately follow the word modified.

Misplaced: Eliot gave *The Waste Land* to his literary executor in manuscript.

Improved: Eliot gave *The Waste Land* in manuscript to his literary executor.

2. Adverbial prepositional phrases should be placed in the sentence so that what they modify is clearly evident.

Misplaced: The editor clarified his position on quoting out of context on Monday.

Improved: On Monday the editor clarified his position on quoting out of context.

c. Subordinate clauses

Misplaced: The Rembrandt was auctioned at the museum, which sold for $1,000,000.

Improved: The Rembrandt, which sold for $1,000,000, was auctioned at the museum.

d. Awkward splitting of verb phrases and infinitives

Awkward: Most students had before coming to college read *The House of the Seven Gables*.

Improved: Most students had read *The House of the Seven Gables* before coming to college.

Awkward: Benjamin Franklin forced himself to again and again copy the prose style of *The Spectator*.

Improved: Benjamin Franklin forced himself again and again to copy the prose style of *The Spectator*.

Gr 12 • *Adjective and Adverb Forms* (adj, adv)

Adjectives and adverbs qualify, limit, make clearer or more specific other words in the sentence. Adjectives modify nouns, pronouns, gerunds, or noun phrases. The suffixes *-al*, *-ish*, *-ive*, *-ly*, *-like* or *-ous* added to nouns form adjectives: *lifelike pose, marvelous time, hoggish manners*.

Adverbs modify verbs (Olivier can play almost any part *perfectly*), adjectives (He was *very* convincing as Hamlet), and other adverbs (Antigone chose death *pitifully* early in life). Adding the suffix *-ly* makes an adverb out of an adjective.

Special Problems

a. Some words that end in *-ly* (*only*) and other words not ending in *-ly* (*slow, quick, straight, little, late, fine*) may be either adjectives or adverbs.

b. Adjectives, not adverbs, are used as complements to the subject. Subject complements follow or precede the verbs *to be, to seem, to become,* and similar verbs, as well as verbs describing the senses: *feel, look, smell, sound,* and *taste*.

> The rock-opera "Tommy" is *vivid* and *compelling*.
> The Who sounded *iconoclastic* on the stage of the Metropolitan Opera House.

In each case the italicized adjective (the complement) modifies the subject. But adverbs are used to describe the action of verbs like *feel* and *taste*.

> He tasted his food *cautiously*.

Use an adjective rather than an adverb when the modifier refers to the direct object—and hence is an objective complement—and not the action of the verb.

> Raise *high* the roofbeam, carpenters!

c. Many nouns are used as adjectives (*picture* show, *television* commercial, *poetry* book). However, to avoid being awkward or ambiguous, use an adjective if an appropriate one is available, or rephrase the sentence.

Awkward: human ecology problems
Better: human ecological problems
Better: problems of human ecology

d. Comparison of adjectives and adverbs (see SS 2a). Adjectives and adverbs have comparative and superlative forms. The comparative form is used to compare two things, the superlative more than two.

Positive	Comparative	Superlative
pretty	prettier	prettiest
naive	more naive	most naive
soon	sooner	soonest
rapid	less rapid	least rapid

King Lear is, perhaps, Shakespeare's *most complex* tragedy (more than two are being compared), but it is *less* often *studied* than *Hamlet* (two are being compared).

Adjectives with one or two syllables usually add the suffixes *-er* and *-est* to form the comparative and superlative; adjectives with more than two syllables and most adverbs use *more, most* or *less, least* with the positive. Some compare either way (greedy, stony). Some adjectives and adverbs have irregular forms in the comparative and superlative degrees.

good well	better	best
little	less	least
much many	more	most
bad	worse	worst

Gr 13 • *Incomplete Constructions* (Inc)

Avoid any incomplete or elliptical construction which leads to awkwardness or confusion. (See P 1d.)

a. Repeat an article or a pronoun before the second word in a compound to indicate the plural.

a novelist and poet (indicates one person)
a novelist and a poet (indicates two people)

    b. Do not omit a conjunction if the omission is likely to cause confusion.

> Marlow saw Kurtz had suffered a grievous change. (The omission of *that* before *Kurtz* causes momentary misreading of the sentence.)

That can be left out if no misreading results.

> Kurtz believed he had found ultimate truth.

    c. Include all prepositions that are needed for sentence clarity.

> Spring they go on pilgrimages. (*In spring* or *each spring*.)

    d. Omission of a verb or a needed auxiliary can cause grammatical and logical inconsistency.

> This theme is relevant and the characters psychologically valid. (*Is* cannot be used for both clauses, since the second has a plural subject.)

    e. Avoid incomplete comparisons; they are awkward and confusing. State the terms of the comparison explicitly.

> The novels of Thomas Wolfe are far more radically original than Hemingway. (Complete the construction by writing *than those of Hemingway*.)

Confusing: Faulkner liked Wolfe better than Hemingway.
Better: Faulkner liked Wolfe better than he liked Hemingway.

    In writing avoid the use of as *so*, *such*, and *too* as intensives without a phrase or clause to complete them.

> Alexander Pope was too deformed. Consequently his satires are so biting. (Substitute *very* or *quite* for *too* and *so*, or better still, use no intensive.)

The *as-good-if-not-better* kind of comparison often causes difficulty.

Awkward: The Sierra Club believes that the population problem is as immediately important, if not more important, than wilderness preservation.
Better: The Sierra Club believes that the population problem is as immediately important as, if not more important than, wilderness preservation.

    Remember this helpful rule: the sentence should make sense if the phrase set off by commas is omitted.

4

Punctuation

P

You can usually get your point across in writing more easily by following, consistently and logically, conventional punctuation.

P 1 • *Period* (.)

a. Use the period at the end of a declarative or imperative statement.

Sherwood Anderson has many psychologically grotesque characters.
You must understand the allusions in T. S. Eliot's poetry.

b. Use a period after some abbreviations.

Dr., Mr., pres., Preston B. Jones, Oct., P.M., U.S.A.

Exception: Some organizations are known by a set of unpunctuated initials: CORE, CIA, AFL-CIO, SEC.

c. Use three spaced periods to indicate editorial omission within a quotation. (See MS 3d.)

d. Spaced periods may be used to indicate suspended or interrupted thought. Since this device is most appropriate for creative writing, it should seldom be used in college themes.

The darkness hung like a heavy curtain . . . no, like a shifting fog . . .
that noise, what is it? . . . thickening fog . . .

P 2 • *Comma* (,)

a. Use the comma to separate main clauses joined by a coordinate conjunction.

> The breeding biology of the Ruff continues to puzzle ornithologists, and no complete explanation of its curious behavior has yet been established.

Exception: Short clauses which are closely related may be joined without the use of the comma.

> The gyrfalcon plunged and the ptarmigan scattered.

b. Use commas to separate items in a series.

> He saw the rich and the poor, the privileged and the oppressed, the powerful and the weak.
> Frankenstein's monster was large, terrifying, and misunderstood.

Note: If no ambiguity results, the comma before *and* may be omitted.

> The great horned owl eats rats, mice and voles.

c. Use commas to separate two minor elements (other than main clauses) not joined by *and*.

> He saw the slowly ascending trail, the forbidding barrier of mountains.

d. Use commas to set off introductory phrases and clauses; however, if a prepositional phrase is short and if no ambiguity results, the comma need not be used.

short prepositional phrase:
> At first Kafka's style is perplexing.

long prepositional phrase:
> In the beginning of Kafka's symbolic novel *The Castle*, the narrated events seem mysteriously dislocated.

introductory verbal phrases:
> To enjoy reading this book, you need to be interested in hunting and fishing.
> Having migrated from Surinam, the Cattle Egret has now established itself in the United States.
> Done with youthful dissipation, he lapsed into aged piety.

introductory clauses:

> Until the last sun has set on the last man, the gods will be kept busy.
>
> Because Hemingway was very jealous of his reputation, he sometimes rejected early friends who had helped him along.

e. Use commas to set off nonrestrictive modifiers and appositives. Do not set off restrictive modifiers since they provide necessary identification of the thing modified.

> Love *which is selfish* may be equated with lust.

A nonrestrictive modifier provides additional information but does not identify the thing modified.

> Love, *a common experience*, is the basis for most popular songs.

An appositive is a noun or noun substitute which provides additional information.

> *Moby Dick*, Melville's whaling book, is charged with reverberating symbolism.

f. Use commas to set off parenthetical or interrupting elements.

> The rockfish, also called the striped bass, probably spawns in tidal waters adjoining Chesapeake Bay.
>
> Othello was a victim, we see, of powerful jealousy deriving from great love.
>
> Men, not women, are credited as being logical creatures.
>
> No man, as Mr. Dooley observed, will become governor if he has a grudge against himself.

g. Use commas to set off absolute constructions, which modify an entire clause rather than any one element within the clause.

> The theory of man's innate nobility being disposed of, we may now examine the idea of the state as a product of rationalism.
>
> Marriage with Maude Gonne being impossible, Yeats turned to his poetry as a restorative.

h. Use commas to set off quoted material or dialogue.

> Shakespeare said, "All the world's a stage."
>
> Joyce's *Portrait of the Artist* begins, "Once upon a time. . . ."

i. Use commas with dates, addresses, and numbers.

On October 14, 1922, she met Cosmo.

Faulkner's home was in Oxford, Mississippi

The country has a population of 203,427,895.

j. Use commas for clarity. Sometimes a comma will prevent an ambiguity or misreading.

Awkward: To a man beating a horse is repugnant.

Clearer: To a man, beating a horse is repugnant.

k. Avoid unnecessary commas.
  1. Do not use a comma between compound elements.
   (a) Unnecessary separation of compound subject:

William Shakespeare, and Ben Jonson were writing at the time of the accession of James I.

   (b) Unnecessary separation of compound verb:

He saw her picture, and wished to marry her.

   (c) Unnecessary separation of compound adjectives:

Truffaut's *Mississippi Mermaid*, which stars Belmondo and which depicts a series of picaresque escapades, received mixed critical reviews.

  2. Do not use an unnecessary comma between closely related elements.
   (a) Unnecessary separation of subject and verb:

The transcendent beauty and grace of Maude Gonne, will exist imperishably in Yeats' poetry.

   (b) Unnecessary separation of verb and object:

Scientists in the eighteenth century seriously believed, that swallows hibernated during the winter.

  3. Do not use commas with restrictive modifiers. (See P 2e.)

André Gide, who won the Nobel Prize, was a very influential French novelist and essayist.

The poet who won the Nobel Prize was born in Italy.

P 3 • *Semicolon* (;)

The semicolon is stronger than a comma (that is, it indicates a longer or more distinct pause), not as strong as a period. The semicolon is used to separate larger elements, often when conjunctions are omitted or when those elements have internal punctuation.

a. Use a semicolon to join independent clauses when the coordinate conjunction is omitted.

War cares nothing for youth and beauty; it feeds on supple flesh and rich blood.

b. Use a semicolon between independent clauses joined by a conjunctive adverb. Conjunctive adverbs (*for example, nevertheless, however, moreover, consequently, therefore*) are not strong enough to make the full connection between independent clauses.

Jefferson loved science and might have chosen to devote his life to it; however, he yielded to a sense of duty, giving himself largely to public service.

c. Use a semicolon to separate clauses and other elements containing internal punctuation.

George, Hortense, and Freddie came at three, staying until eight; but Frances, who arrived at four, did not leave till ten.

He ate bread, cheese, and beef; drank beer, wine and gin; and loved blondes, brunettes, and redheads.

He loved good foods—ripe cheeses, fat shrimp, loins of beef; strong drink—rich ale, fortified wines, and all varieties of distilled spirits; and lovely women of all descriptions.

P 4 • *Colon* (:)

The colon is a strong linking mark, used most often when a statement is brought to a point of expectation. The material after the colon satisfies that expectation.

a. Use a colon preceding a statement which clearly enlarges upon what has gone before.

I know what America needs: a dedication to some principle other than materialism, to some pursuit other than the good life as prophesied by Hugh Hefner.

b. Use a colon to introduce elements following a complete statement. With an incomplete statement the colon is unnecessary.

Incomplete: In the South Seas, Melville saw: primitive tribes, misguided missionaries, and the early inroads of civilization.

Complete: He brought home a number of interesting souvenirs: harpoons, vials of coconut oil, scrimshaw, and wooden domestic utensils.

c. A colon may be used to introduce a quotation.

He argued: "But Milton's purpose in *Paradise Lost* is indeed lofty. He tries to 'justifie the ways of God to men.' "

P 5 • *Question Mark* (?)

Use a question mark at the end of an interrogative utterance.

Who came to see you? Why? When?
Someone (was it Raquel?) slipped away before dawn.

If a sentence is a combination of declarative and interrogative clauses, the clause at the end determines the punctuation.

The Faerie Queene is in many ways a dull poem; how many people have voluntarily read the entire work?

How many people have read all of *The Faerie Queene* and enjoyed it; it is, after all, in many ways quite dull.

P 6 • *Exclamation Point* (!)

Use the exclamation mark sparingly for utterances that are clearly exclamatory. Overuse of the exclamation mark seems artificial and forced. In the following example, however, the emotional situation justifies the punctuation.

The woman yelled, "Help! My God, he's been shot!"

P 7 • *Dash* (—)

Dashes, like commas and parentheses, are used to set off parenthetical, explanatory, or interrupting elements. Since the dash is the strongest of the three marks, it should be used where the interruption is pronounced, where the element to be set off needs strong emphasis, or where the element to be set off has internal commas.

Note that the dash is physically longer than the hyphen. When typing, use two hyphens to make a dash.

> Melville—perhaps you are not aware of this—wrote a long poem called *Clarel*.

> In modern British history, one man stands eminently as the great leader—Winston Churchill.

> We must do our best—in economic aid, in rational foreign policy, and in the enlightened use of power—to make certain that emerging nations become substantial free states.

P 8 • *Quotation Marks* (")

(See also MS 3f, for the use of quotation marks with other punctuation marks.)

a. Use quotation marks to indicate dialogue or material directly quoted.

> "I'll see you later," John said.
> "When?" asked Reginald.
> "Oh," he replied, "in ten, maybe twenty, years."

> Jonathan Edwards, the Puritan theologian and preacher, felt himself to be a creature of sin: "My wickedness, as I am in myself, has long appeared to me perfectly ineffable, and swallowing up all thought and imagination. . . ."

b. Use quotation marks for the titles of short works. (See MS 1.)

P 9 • *Parentheses* ( )

a. Use parentheses to enclose parenthetical, incidental, or supplementary material. Notice especially the punctuation in the following examples.

Ben Jonson (1572-1637), who admired the classical dramatic models, was one of Shakespeare's great rivals in the London theater.

Ben Franklin (everyone knows the story) used the kite and key for his most famous experiment.

When you take an examination, bring the usual materials (pen and ink, loose-leaf paper, and a functioning brain).

　　b. Use parentheses to enclose notations when items are being listed or enumerated.

The student should ask himself several basic questions about a poem: (1) Who speaks in the poem? (2) What are the dramatic circumstances of that speaker? (3) Is the speaker the poet, a mask for the poet, or an imaginary character distinct from the poet?

A theme has a three-part construction: (a) the introduction, (b) the body, with its divisions, and (c) the summary or conclusion.

P 10 • *Brackets* [ ]

　　Use brackets within quoted matter for editorial insertions; that is, indicate matter which is not part of the original by enclosing it within brackets. (See also MS 3e.)

Poe addresses Science as the "true daughter of Old Time [that is, time as a destroyer] . . . / Who alterest all things with thy peering eyes."

In *Ligeia* the narrator says, "I well remember something in a volume by Joseph Glanvill [1636-1680], which (perhaps merely from its quaintness—who shall say?) never failed to inspire me. . . ."

Note: Do not confuse the use of brackets and parentheses. The date above in brackets would be an editorial insertion; the statement in parentheses was written by Poe.

5

Spelling

Sp

English spelling is difficult because it is often neither logical nor consistent. A dictionary provides the best help; have one near when you are writing a theme. For more severe problems try one of the several books on the subject.

Sp 1 • *Apostrophe* (')

Use the apostrophe:

a. To form the possessive case of nouns and some indefinite pronouns:

a day's pay, Eliot's "Sweeney Agonistes," a boy's will, everyone's dilemma.

Special Problems

1. Add an apostrophe and an *s* to form the possessive of singular or plural nouns that do not end in an *s* or *z* sound.

one man's family
several men's families

2. Add only the apostrophe when the plural ends in an *s* or *z* sound: writers' schools. Many organizations omit the apostrophe in their names: Cotton Producers Association.

3. Add an apostrophe and an *s* to one-syllable words if the singular ends in an *s* or *z* sound. For words of more than one syllable, usually add only the apostrophe unless the final *s* sound is pronounced.

Burns's poems, Oedipus' curse

4. With compounds or nouns in joint possession, add the apostrophe to the last word. To show individual possession make each noun possessive.

the rank-and-file's opinion
Abercrombie and Fitch's catalog
Wordsworth and Coleridge's *Lyrical Ballads* (joint authorship)
Wordsworth's and Coleridge's poems (separate authorship)

b. To form contractions (not usually appropriate for college themes and formal writing).

You're (you are), she's (she is), doesn't (does not), it's (it is)

c. To show that a number has been omitted (again, usually too informal for most themes).

the feminine '50's
the class of '70

d. To form plurals of numbers, letters, and words being discussed as words.

Mind your *p's* and *q's*
You use too many *this's*
Have you noticed how frequently *9's* appear in advertising copy?

Sp 2 • *Hyphen* (-)

Use a hyphen:

a. With compound words:

self-aggrandizement, love-hate relationship.

At any one time there may be a wide variety of acceptable practices in hyphenating or not hyphenating compounds. Check an up-to-date dictionary for current usage.

Many compound nouns are hyphenated when they are used as adjectives: an off-the-cuff remark, a holier-than-thou attitude.

b. With compound numbers from twenty-one to ninety-nine.

c. With words that must be separated at the end of lines. Always divide a word between syllables or parts such as prefixes and suffixes. The dictionary is your authority for syllable division. Do not divide a word of only one syllable and do not separate one letter from the rest of the word. Separate hyphenated words at the hyphen. (See also MS 8.)

d. With the prefixes *ex-* (meaning "former"), *self-*, *all-*, *quasi-*, and sometimes *co-*, and the suffix *-elect*.

ex-wife, self-righteous, all-knowing, President-elect, co-author

e. With prefixes before words that are capitalized.

anti-American, pro-German

f. With prefixes when the second word begins with the same vowel with which the first ends.

anti-intellectual, re-entry

g. With words that have identical prefixes with different meanings.

depress/de-press, recreation/re-creation

Sp 3 • *Plurals*

Form the plural by adding *s* to the singular except when the plural is pronounced with an additional syllable, in which case add *-es*.

book, books
box, boxes

Consult the special section in your dictionary on the formation of irregular plurals.

Special Problems

1. Form the plural of nouns that end in *y* preceded by a consonant by changing the *y* to *i* and adding *es*:

tragedy, tragedies
century, centuries

If the final *y* is preceded by a vowel, merely add an *s*:

journey, journeys
boy, boys

2. Form the plural of nouns ending in *fe* by changing the *fe* to *ve* and adding *s*:

wife, wives

Some nouns that end in *f* change the *f* to *v* and add *es*:

leaf, leaves

3. Some nouns that end in *o* take the *es* plural even though the plural does not require an extra syllable:

hero, heroes
Negro, Negroes
tomato, tomatoes

4. To form the plural of compound words, usually add the *s* to the main word:

mothers-in-law
ladies-in-waiting

5. Many foreign words retain their plural forms:

syllabus, syllabi
stadium, stadia
curriculum, curricula
alumnus, alumni

Frequently when the word becomes standard English the foreign plural is dropped or becomes an alternative spelling:

gymnasium, gymnasiums, gymnasia
cactus, cactuses, cacti
fungus, fungi, funguses

Sp 4 • *Capitalization*

a. Capitalize proper nouns and adjectives formed from them.

John Burroughs, Canada, Scully Square
Wordsworthian, Canadian, Elizabethan

Derivatives of proper names occasionally lose their particularity and thus are not capitalized.

panic from *Pan, sadism,* from the *Marquis de Sade, spartan* from Sparta

Some words may be used as either common names or proper names.

a democratic form of government, the Democratic party

b. Capitalize generic names like mountain, river, street, school, park, captain, and president (of a country) when they are used with a proper noun.

Rocky Mountains, Victoria Falls, Park Avenue, Shenandoah Valley, Skyros Island, Captain Carpenter, Central Park, Summerhill School, Norris Lake

c. Capitalize the first words of sentences, direct quotations, lines of poetry, and footnotes.

The seige of Leningrad failed.
He mumbled, "Are you sure?"
"Heard melodies are sweet, but those unheard are sweeter." (Line from "Ode on a Grecian Urn.")

d. Capitalize the pronoun *I*.

My cousin and I were lucky to reach Woodstock.

e. Capitalize words that indicate family relationships when not preceded by articles or possessive pronouns.

Mother and Father won't tolerate long hair.

f. Capitalize titles that precede a proper noun.

Secretary Hickel, Mr. Percy, Dr. Bernard, Justice Douglas, Queen Elizabeth

g. Capitalize the words in titles except articles, prepositions, and conjunctions. Frequently long prepositions and conjunctions are also capitalized. Always capitalize the first and last words of titles.

A Hall of Mirrors, The Memoirs of George Sherston, "A Rose for Emily," *The Voyage of the Beagle*, *Men Without Women*

h. Capitalize the names of races and ethnic groups, but not economic or social groups.

Negro, Slav, Caucasian, Jew, the bourgeoisie

i. Capitalize the names of historical events and periods.

The Battle of Waterloo, the Enlightenment, the Middle Ages

j. Capitalize the points of the compass when they refer to regions rather than directions.

Fitzgerald came from the Midwest.
Go three paces north and two west.

k. Capitalize the titles of specific courses.

Math 101, Sociology 499

l. Capitalize the names of seasons when they refer to school quarters or semesters.

the Summer Quarter

m. Capitalize the names of some military organizations, departments and committees, and philosophical or political systems.

the Air Force, Research Department, Blue Ribbon Committee, Communism, War on Poverty, Peace Corps

n. Capitalize the first word of a sentence in parentheses when it stands alone but not when it is within another sentence.

Henry Miller's novels have gained a certain respectability (they are even assigned as required reading in some college courses), to the great dismay of the author.

Henry Miller's novels, to his great dismay, have gained a certain respectability. (They are even assigned as required reading in some college courses.)

o. Capitalize the names and abbreviations of associations, clubs, and other organizations.

the Lions Club	CIO
YMCA	Phi Beta Kappa
SDS	United Daughters of the Confederacy (U.D.C.)

p. Capitalize sacred names.

the Bible, the Old Testament, the Koran, Talith, the Messiah, the Cross

Sp 5 • *Spelling Rules*

In English, spelling and pronunciation frequently do not match. English spelling is neither regular nor logical. Letters can stand for a confusing number of sounds, and the same sound can be spelled in a number of ways: sky, high; women, fish. To further confuse matters, many words have letters that are not pronounced: psyche, know, write. And homonyms sound alike but differ in spelling: peace–piece, principal-principle.

Correct spelling is always a problem. Careless misspellings can be caught by painstaking proofreading: always check the finished copy before turning a paper in. Get in the habit of consulting a dictionary on any word you are unsure of.

Although the spelling of many words is illogical and must simply be memorized, a few spelling rules, despite many exceptions, can provide some help.

a. *ie and ei.* The *i* usually comes before the *e* except after *c* or when pronounced as *a* (as in eight): *conceive, relieve, niece, siege, neighbor, reign, ceiling.* However, there are many exceptions: *ei*ther, w*ei*rd, sp*ec*ies.

b. *Final e.* Usually a final *e* is omitted before a suffix beginning with a vowel and retained before a suffix beginning with a consonant. *Awful, truly, singeing, argument,* and *hoeing* are among the exceptions.

bore–boring–boredom	rude–rudeness
like–likeable–likely	come–coming
prime–primary	love–lovable–lovely
care–careful	fame–famous

The final *e* following *c* or *g* is retained before suffixes beginning with *a* or *o*.

noticeable, outrageous, vengeance, courageous

c. *Consonants before suffixes.* When adding a suffix beginning with a vowel to a word ending in a single consonant preceded by an accented vowel, double the final consonant. Do not double the final consonant if it is preceded by a double vowel or if the preceding vowel is not accented.

stop—stopped	help—helped
plan—planned	forget—forgetting
begin—beginning	keep—keeper

d. *Final y.* A final *y* changes to *i* when a suffix is added.

dry—drier	busy—business
noisy—noisily	study—studious
library—libraries	

But when a vowel precedes the *y* or when the suffix begins with an *i* the *y* does not change.

scurry—scurrying   play—played

Exceptions: day—daily, say—said

e. *Prefix ending in same letter that begins root word.* When a prefix ends in the same letter that begins the root word, both are retained.

unnoticed	irreplaceable	misspelling
unnecessary	immobile	

Sp 6 • *Frequently misspelled words*

Several groups of words cause special difficulty in spelling.

a. Some words are so frequently mispronounced that they are also misspelled: *privlege* for *privilege, mischievious* for *mischievous, tempermental* for *temperamental, athaletics* for *athletics, libary* for *library*. In speech the final *ed* is often dropped or slurred, leading to misspellings such as *use to* for *used to, middle age* for *middle aged*, and *old fashion* for *old fashioned*.

b. Words ending in *able* and *ible* are frequently confused. *Able* endings far outnumber *ible* ones.

irresistible	plausible
acceptable	horrible
capable	terrible
suitable	forceable

c. The endings *ance, ant, ence,* and *ent* are not distinguished by sound and hence are often confused in spelling.

excellence	existence	experience
acceptance	excellent	respondent
performance	independent	persistent

d. A number of words that sound alike cause confusion.

accept—except	lead—led
adopt—adapt	loose—lose
allusion—illusion	moral—morale
censor—censure	peace—piece
coarse—course	personal—personnel
complement—compliment	precede—proceed
choose—chose	principal—principle
conscience—conscious	stationary—stationery
consul—council—counsel	statue—statute
effect—affect	than—then
formally—formerly	to—too—two
later—latter	who's—whose

e. Some words present the question of whether they are spelled as one word or two.

all ready—already (adverb)
all right—alright (nonstandard)
all together—altogether (adverb meaning wholly)
a while—awhile (adverb)
may be (verb phrase)—maybe (adverb)

f. Words with silent or slurred letters often cause misspelling.

February, environment, probably, literature, doubt, condemn, candidate, usually

g. The following list consists of words commonly misspelled.

absence	candidate	embarrass
abundance	category	eminent
accidentally	certain	endeavor
accommodate	changeable	enforce
accumulate	clothes	entertain
accuracy	coarse	environment
accuse	column	equipped
achievement	comfortable	erroneous
acquaint	coming	especially
acquire	commercial	exaggerate
acquitted	committee	exceed
adequate	comparative	excellent
adolescence	competitive	exhaust
aggravate	concede	existence
aisle	conceive	experience
already	conquer	extreme
altogether	conscience	
always	conscious	familiar
among	controversy	fantasy
analysis	criticism	fascinate
analyze		February
anxiety	dealt	fictitious
apparent	deceit	financial
appearance	definite	foreign
argument	describe	formerly
article	despair	forty
ascend	desperate	fulfill
attendance	device	
athlete	difference	gaiety
audience	dilemma	generally
	disastrous	genius
basically	discrimination	government
beautiful	dissatisfied	grammar
becoming	divine	grievous
beginning	dominant	guidance
beneficial		
breathe	ecstasy	handled
brilliant	efficient	height
Britain	eighth	heroine
business	eliminate	hindrance

huge
humorous
hurriedly
hypocrisy

imaginary
incidentally
inevitable
influential
ingenious
initiative
instance
instants
intelligent
intercede
interest
interpret
irrelevant

its
it's

jealousy

knowledge

laboratory
later
latter
lead
led
leisure
library
license
literary
loose
lose
losing
luxury

maintenance
maneuver
manufacturer
marriage
meant
mechanics

medicine
melancholy
mere
miniature
minute
mischievous
misspelled
monotonous
moral
morale
muscle
mysterious

naive
naturally
necessary
Negroes
neither
niece
ninety
ninth
noble
noticeable

obstacle
occasion
occurred
omitted
operate
opinion
oppose
opportunity
optimistic
original

pamphlets
parallel
paralyzed
parliament
particular
pastime
perform
perhaps
permanent
permissible

persistent
personnel
phase
playwright
political
possession
precede
predominant
preference
prejudice
presence
prestige
prevalent
principal
principle
privilege
probably
proceed
pronunciation
propaganda
prophecy
psychic
psychology
pursuit

quantity
quiet

realize
rebel
receive
recognize
recommend
referring
regard
relative
relieve
religion
repetition
representative
resemblance
response
rhythm
ridicule
roommate

sacrifice
sacrilegious
schedule
secretary
seize
sense
separate
sergeant
shepherd
significance
similar
sophomore
strictly
studying
success
summarize
surprise
susceptible
suspense

technique
temperament
themselves
tendency
therefore
thorough
thought
till
tragedy
transferred
trouble
truly
tyranny

undoubtedly
unnecessary
until
useful
usually

vacuum
valuable
vegetable
vengeance
villain

warrant
weak
Wednesday
weird
whether
whole
whose
writing
written

yield
your
you're

6

Diction and Style

D

D 1 • *Levels of Usage*

Language, like clothing and behavior, should fit the occasion. Formal usage is no more or less correct than informal usage, only more or less appropriate. The writer's problem is to know not only which level of usage to employ, but also how to remain on that level or when to shift to another level to achieve some special effect. Shifts in levels of usage should be made sparingly and knowingly.

The three basic levels of language usage are formal, informal or colloquial, and substandard or nonstandard.

a. *Formal Usage*. Formal language has dignity, precision, and at its best, grace. It is the usual language of religious ritual, commencement addresses, political documents, textbooks, presidential addresses, official reports, and the like where precision is the most important consideration. A naive misconception supported by much bad writing is that formal language is by its very nature stiff and dull.

The basic level of academic writing is formal, but many college themes will be informal. An instructor should indicate the level or levels of usage he expects his students to employ. When in doubt, ask.

b. *Informal or Colloquial Usage*. The term *informal* relates to written language; *colloquial*, to spoken language. However, *colloquial* is often applied to writing which captures the flavor of speech. Both terms describe a casual, relaxed manner.

Formal: His style is inflated.

Informal: He uses his writing to show off all the big words he knows.

c. *Substandard or Nonstandard Usage.* Substandard or nonstandard language includes those categories of words which ordinarily should be avoided in formal writing: slang, obscenities, coinages, and expressions which are illiterate, dialectal, archaic, or obsolete. At times, of course, nonstandard expressions can be used with good effect. An obscentity can suggest strong feeling. An archaism can be savory. Coinages are often fresh and witty. Although in college writing formal usage is the norm, the student should not feel restricted by any rule which prevents effective communication.

D 2 • Slang

Slang should be used rarely and for specific effects. Slang can be earthy, vivid, and fresh. It is highly contemporary language, shifting and evolving rapidly, and therefore it gives the impression that one is in touch with current culture. On the negative side, because slang is contemporary, it dates quickly. As the language of insiders, slang can be an impediment to communication with outsiders. The overuse of slang tends to vagueness and monotony.

Examples:

cool (knowledgeable, desirable, admirable, fine)

fuzz (police)

to take a trip (to be under the influence of a drug or narcotic)

to bust a course (to fail a course)

straight (conventional, stolid)

to beef (to complain)

to rap (to talk with)

zip (nothing)

D 3 • Dialect

Dialect (also sometimes referred to as localisms or provincialisms) is language characteristic of a geographical area. Use it sparingly and knowledgeably in formal writing and college themes.

Examples:

to shuck off one's clothing (Southeastern; to take off one's clothing)

near (New England; frugal)

shorthorn (Western; an inexperienced person)

poke (Southeastern; a sack or bag)

D 4 • *Illiteracies*

Avoid illiteracies; these are usages typical of an uneducated person.
Examples:

He *warn't* here.
He *don't* like *nobody*.
They fixed it *theirselves*.

D 5 • *Concreteness*

Whenever possible, use concrete rather than vague or abstract language.
Vague, generalized diction is dull; specific, concrete language is more lively,
more interesting. Verbs as well as nouns should be vivid. Active verbs are
stronger than passive verbs.
Examples:

Vague: The book was dull.
Concrete: Mindless repetition and totally predictable characters made the book
stupefying reading.

General: We are confronted by many grave issues.
More specific: The nation yearns to resolve the problems of racial disharmony,
poverty within general abundance, and the deterioration of the cities.

Passive: *Mash* and *Catch-22* were termed bizarrely comic by the critics.
Active: Critics termed *Mash* and *Catch-22* bizarrely comic.

D 6 • *Exactness*

Choose words which convey your meaning precisely.
Formal expository prose should not merely allow the reader to see what is
meant; it should make it impossible to misunderstand. The student should
cultivate two important and useful habits: use of the dictionary to find the exact
word and careful rewriting. Practiced writers know that the first word which
comes to mind is not always the exact word and that the only way to get exact
words in smooth order is by conscientiously using the dictionary and laboriously
revising.

D 7 • *Wordiness and Repetition*

Omit words which are not necessary for clarity and smoothness.

Once you have written the first draft of a paper, chances are your main problem in revising will be cutting away. Just as we often talk while waiting for the thought to emerge, so in writing we also tend to put down needless words, desperately hoping that we can capture the idea. But the idea may become smothered in excessive and repetitious verbiage.

Examples:

Wordy: The time when she came to see me. I was sick in bed with pneumonia. That was the last time in my life that I talked with her.

Improved: She came to see me while I had pneumonia. That was our last conversation.

Repetitious and wordy: The problems of the city are problems to the resolution of which we must apply all of our resources.

Improved: We must use our talent and wealth to solve the problems of the city.

D 8 • *Jargon*

Unless you are writing for a specialized audience, avoid jargon.

Jargon, as the term is used here, means the technical or professional language of specialized activities. This language can be very effective when used among insiders, but baffling to the uninitiated. You should not use jargon unless there is no better language for a technical subject; then you should define all terms which may be obscure to the general reader. (*Jargon* is also used sometimes to mean inflated language; see D 9.)

In writing for a general audience, terms such as the following should be avoided or defined:

Mimus polyglottos (mockingbird)

amphimacher (a type of metrical foot in versification)

genitourinary (having to do with the functions or organs of procreation and urination)

mandamus (a judicial directive ordering certain actions)

sheets (in sailing, ropes)

D 9 • *Inflated Language*

Be as simple and direct as you can.

Inflated language is ponderous, elaborately constructed, full of words, and often empty of content. It is an easy shield for the writer who wants to sound knowledgeable but has little to say.

Example:

Inflated: The leadership factor in personnel of administrative status or higher is of determining importance in the actualization of projects established through policy directives and also of those which are self-initiated by such personnel; personnel of administrative position must motivate personnel in subordinate positions in order that desired results be obtained with maximum efficiency and minimum inefficiency.

Deflated: An administrator must be a leader in order to get his subordinates to work well.

D 10 • *Clichés*

Avoid clichés.

Clichés (trite, dully familiar, hackneyed expressions) give the effect of a tired mind treating a stale subject. They cannot stimulate or interest the reader. Since clichés offer themselves so readily to the writer, they often must be taken out in your revision. Find a fresh way to convey your meaning.

Examples:

tried and true	crazy as a loon	it's a small world
last but not least	crazy like a fox	a crucial play
ships passing in the night	the long arm of the law	down but not out
my heart's desire	high as a kite	a clutch player

D 11 • *Idioms*

Use idiomatic expressions properly.

An idiom is an expression which cannot be explained by the logic of grammar or which has a meaning distinct from the collected meaning of its separate words. Idioms cause extreme difficulties for non-native users of a language, but even native speakers of English have trouble with the idiomatic use of some prepositions. Notice the shifts of meaning in the following lists:

get around, get after, get even, get over;

put about, put across, put away, put down, put in, put off, put on, put out, put over.

Examples of troublesome idiomatic prepositions:

to be covetous *of*
to be oblivious *of*
to be indifferent *to*
to be angry *with* a person, angry *at* or *about* a thing

D 12 • *Denotation and Connotation*

Be aware of the connotation as well as the denotation of words.

Denotation is the literal or basic meaning of an expression. Connotation is the subtler shades of attitude and association attached to a word. Words which refer to adult females, for instance, have widely varying connotations: *lady, dame, broad, doll, bird,* and *woman.* Context often determines connotation; *capitalism* as used on Wall Street implies an attitude far different from *capitalism* as used in statements by the government of Red China. As John Brodie said, "When I throw the ball quickly they say I dumped it; when Namath throws it they say he has a quick release."

Further examples:

kill, slay, exterminate, liquidate
freedom, laxity, liberty, license
thin, slim, skinny, gaunt
employee, worker, hireling
rural area, backwoods
plump, chubby, fat, overweight
colorful, unusual, eccentric, different

D 13 • *Figurative Language*

Use figures of speech which are consistent and appropriate.

The basic figures of speech are similes, metaphors, personifications, understatement, and overstatement.

A *simile* is an overt comparison, often using *like* or *as*:

"They came like swallows and like swallows went."

A *metaphor* is also a comparison but is stated as if one thing were the other:

"An aged man is but a paltry thing,/A tattered coat upon a stick.
..."

A *personification* (a type of metaphor) endows nonhuman objects with human characteristics:

"Cruelty has a human heart,/ And jealousy a human face. . . ."

Understatement operates by saying that a thing is less than it is, thereby indirectly calling attention to the true proportions of the object:

"One could do worse than be a swinger of birches."

Overstatement (hyperbole) exaggerates to be emphatic or, used sarcastically, to deflate.

"An hundred years should go to praise
Thine eyes, and on thy forehead gaze."

Your backhand is as good as Arthur Ashe's. (This overstatement, depending on the circumstances and the tone of delivery, could be praise or criticism.)

Figures of comparison can lose their effect through inappropriateness or inconsistency. In praising the loyalty of an admirable man, one would not use a comparison with the loyalty of a dog, since a dog's loyalty involves no independence of mind or spirit. Shifting too rapidly from one figure to another can also jar the reader: "She wound him around her little finger like putty and discarded him like an old shoe." "Keep your shoulder to the wheel and your nose to the ground."

7

Library Papers
LP

The college student from time to time has to write papers requiring the use of library materials. These papers are commonly referred to as library papers, research papers, or term papers. After their freshman year, most students find that they are expected to know how to present research without additional instruction. Obviously, then, the freshman should think of the library paper as an introduction to a method, not as a task to be done once and then forgotten.

GENERAL STEPS IN WRITING THE LIBRARY PAPER

LP 1 • *Getting the topic*

If you have a choice, make every effort to get a topic which interests you. Be certain that the topic you settle on is suitable for the assigned length of your paper. Students have great difficulty in narrowing a topic sufficiently. One might, for example, wish to write about William Faulkner. If the assignment were a critical paper of 3500 words, it would be impossible to cover much ground. So you might elect Faulkner's attitute toward Negroes. But that is still too broad. The student then might narrow the topic to Faulkner's treatment of Negroes in one or two novels or in a few short stories. But if the paper required intensive analysis, you might do well to write on the treatment of Negroes in a single short story.

LP 2 • *Making the working bibliography*

Your instructor will suggest places to look for materials on your topic. You should become familiar with the Library's card catalogue and with basic

70

reference and bibliographical sources. As you read about your subject, you will find references to further sources which you should check. Each time you find reference to an item of possible use, make a bibliography card. The working bibliography is your collection of cards (3 X 5 cards are handy) on which you record appropriate information about each source. Be certain that the bibliography card has full information in the same form you will use in making your finished bibliography; it is easier to do it exactly the first time. (See MS 5 in the next chapter for bibliography forms.)

Below is a selective listing of basic resources likely to be of use to a college student writing a library paper.

Information on Reference Resources

Constance M. Winchell. *Guide to Reference Books*. 8th ed. Chicago: American Library Association, 1967.

General Guide to Essays

Essay and General Literature Index, 1900-1933. (With Supplements to the present.)

General Guide to Periodical Articles

Readers' Guide to Periodical Literature. (Published monthly and accumulated into volumes.)

Biographical Reference

Dictionary of American Biography. (With Supplements.)
Dictionary of National Biography. (For British subjects. With Supplements.)
Webster's Biographical Dictionary. (Not restricted by nationality.)

News Index

The New York Times Index. (Published monthly; accumulated into annual volumes.)

English and American Literature

Richard D. Altick and Andrew Wright. *Selective Bibliography for the Study of English and American Literature*. New York: The Macmillan Company, 1960.

Literary Handbook

William Flint Thrall and Addison Hibbard. *A Handbook to Literature*. Rev. and enl. by C. Hugh Holman. New York: The Odyssey Press, Inc., 1960.

Literary History

Albert C. Baugh et al. *A Literary History of England*. New York: Appleton-Century-Crofts, 1948.
Robert E. Spiller et al. *Literary History of the United States*. 3 vols. New York: The Macmillan Company, 1948. Bibliographical Supplement, 1962.

Bibliography of Literary Scholarship

The Annual Bibliography in *PMLA*.
The Quarterly Bibliography in *American Literature*.
Lewis Leary. *Articles on American Literature, 1900-1950*. Durham, N.C.; Duke University Press, 1954.
Lewis Leary, with Carolyn Bartholet and Catharine Roth. *Articles on American Literature, 1950-1967*. Durham, N.C.: Duke University Press, 1970.

LP 3 • *Taking notes*

As you read, make notes on your cards. Use a separate card for each note. Take copious notes, on the assumption that you want to have everything you could conceivably use in writing the paper. You will, of course, finally discard many of the notes, but you will not know which to use and which to discard until you actually write the paper.

Each note card should contain (a) a heading indicating the subject of the note, (b) a brief identification of the source of the note, (c) the page or pages from which the note was taken, and (d) the note itself, which may be a direct quotation, a paraphrase, a summary, or a combination of the three. In addition, you often should record your thoughts on the material dealt with on the note card. However, be certain to distinguish clearly between material from a source and your own ideas.

Sample Note Card

		Subject heading
	Melville's plan to write <u>Pierre</u>	
Source	Melville, <u>Letters</u>, p. 146	
Quotation	"But, My Dear Lady. I shall not again send you a bowl of salt water. The next chalice I shall command, will be a rural bowl of milk."	
Reaction of the note-taker	(Did Melville mean that his next book would be a sweet and gentle pastoral novel?)	

The body of the note card is a direct quotation from Merrell R. Davis and William H. Gilman, eds., The Letters of Herman Melville *(New Haven and London: Yale University Press, 1960), p. 146.*

LP 4 • *Making the outline*

Whether or not you are required to, you should make an outline before writing a first draft. Formulating a clear outline is a major step in achieving an orderly paper. Even when you find yourself revising and rearranging your outline, you still are likely to be working with an organized set of materials.

Preparatory to making an outline, thumb through your note cards. Jot down topics which seem of major importance. See if those major topics can be ordered into the main divisions of your paper; if so, make a stack of cards for each of the divisions. Then work out the subtopics within each stack of cards. Next, try a rough outline. If the outline seems good, you can begin to write.

You will probably use either a topic outline or a sentence outline. Once you have chosen to use topical headings (e.g., "Melville's plan for *Pierre*") or sentence entries (e.g., "Melville hoped that *Pierre* would be a commercial success"), you must remain consistent. Try to use parallel construction in your entries, since parallel form logically suggests parallel ideas. For example, "The Plan of *Pierre*" and "The Reception of *Pierre*" are parallel in form, but "The

Plan of *Pierre*" and *"Pierre's* Reception" are not. Also, follow conventional notation, making certain each entry has at least one other parallel entry. Since a subheading indicates a division of material or idea, a single subtopic is illogical: nothing has been divided. Note the form in the following sample topic outline.

SATIRE IN SINCLAIR LEWIS'S BABBITT

I. Satire of the Business World
  A. Satire of the hero
    1. Babbitt's ethics
      a. his attitude toward himself
      b. his attitude toward others
    2. Babbitt's actions
      a. his shady deals
      b. his temporary rebellion
  B. Satire of minor characters
    1. Virgil Gunch
    2. Chum Frink
    3. John Jennison Drew
II. Satire of the Social World
  A. Babbitt's family relations
    1. His relationship with Myra
    2. His relationship with his children
  B. Babbitt's external social relations
    1. His relationship with his business associates
    2. His relationship with his neighbors
    3. His relationship with "The Bunch"

LP 5 • *Writing and revising*

Writing a first draft becomes a test of your outline and note-taking. The outline is merely a tool to aid your writing, not a tyrant to be followed slavishly. When the actual writing reveals flaws in the outline, the outline should be reworked. You may find, too, that you did not take enough notes or that the ones you have are incomplete; in either case, you must go back and remedy the fault.

In the first draft you should get everything down, including footnotes. Since cutting out is easier than adding to, the first draft should be on the full side. In second and successive drafts you can cut out and polish. On your next-to-last draft, check all footnotes, quotations, and bibliography entries for absolute accuracy; you can then use that draft for a final check on the accuracy of the finished paper.

8

Mechanics of Manuscripts

MS

MS 1 • *Titles*

a. *Your own title.* Do not use quotation marks or italics for the title of your own paper when it precedes the body of your text. Your title, however, may contain a reference requiring quotation marks or italics, as in the following:

The Background of *Hamlet*

b. *Quotation marks and italics for titles.* The basic convention is that quotation marks are used for the titles of short works or portions of longer works; italics, for longer works or works published separately. (Underline words in script or typing to indicate italics.)

Use quotation marks for the titles of songs, short stories, chapters from books, essays, and articles.

"Yesterday," "The Snows of Kilimanjaro," "The Whiteness of the Whale," "The Knocking on the Gate in *Macbeth*."

Latest usage suggests leaving the initial article (unless it is definitely a part of the title) in roman letters and in lower case unless it begins a sentence.

Use italics for:

1. titles and subtitles of books, pamphlets, plays, and other works published separately.

The Sun Also Rises, A Streetcar Named Desire

2. Newspapers, magazines, journals.

The New York *Times* (or *The New York Times*), *Ramparts, Journal of the American Medical Association*

3. Long musical compositions.

Britten's *War Requiem, West Side Story*

4. Long poems.

Paradise Lost, The Dunciad

5. Foreign words and phrases, but not whole sentences.

I felt a sense of *déjà vu*.
Most people suffer through a period of *sturm und drang*.

Note: Do not use quotation marks or italics for the Bible or its parts.

MS 2 • *Pagination*

Use small roman numerals for the pages of prefatory materials (e.g., outline, preface, table of contents) in a long manuscript. Use arabic numerals for the pages in the body of the text. Ordinarily place a page number at the top center or top right of a page; but on pages which have headings, either omit the page number or center it at the bottom.

MS 3 • *Quotations*

Indicate direct quotation by quotation marks or by setting off the quoted material.

a. *Short quotations*. Short passages taken from a source or quoted dialogue should be placed in quotation marks and incorporated in the text.

Direct quotation: She said, "I'll meet you at the Filmore East at nine."
Quotation from a source: Melville's *Moby Dick* begins, "Call me Ishmael."
Quotation from a poem: In Stevens' "Sunday Morning," the speaker wonders, "Is there no change of fruit in paradise?/Does ripe fruit never fall?"

Note: Two lines or less of poetry may be quoted in your text. Use a slash mark, as in the example above, to indicate the break at the end of a line.

b. *Long quotations.* Longer passages should be set off from the text. Set off ten lines or more of prose, two lines or more of poetry. Setting off indicates quotation, so do not add quotation marks to the original; however, retain all quotation marks in the original. A blocked prose quotation should be set in five spaces from the left margin; poetry should be centered on the page. Your text will be double spaced. Skip an additional line before and after a blocked quotation; single space within the quotation.

c. *Quotations within quotations.* Use double quotation marks to begin a quotation, single quotation marks for a quotation within quoted matter. If additional sets of marks are needed, continue the alternation of double and single marks.

William said, "I heard you say, 'George asked, "Where?" ' "

d. *Ellipses, or omissions from quotations.* Use ellipsis marks (three spaced dots or periods) to indicate an omission within quoted material. Make certain that you include punctuation required for sense or sentence structure.

Ishmael says, "Some years ago . . . [,] having little or no money in my purse, and nothing in particular to interest me on shore, I thought I would sail about a little. . . ."

Note: The inserted comma, necessary for sense, is placed in brackets, indicating that it is not in the original. At the end of the quotation, three dots indicate that the sentence continues in the original; the fourth dot is required end punctuation. If several lines are omitted from a set-off quotation, the omission is indicated by a full line of spaced periods.

O, that this too too solid flesh would melt,
Thaw, and resolve itself into a dew!

. . . .

O God! O God!
How weary, stale, flat, and unprofitable,
Seems to me all the uses of this world!

e. *Brackets for matter inserted within a quotation.* Punctuation or phrasing inserted within a quotation must be placed in brackets. (*Note*: Do not use parentheses for editiorial insertions.)

"And when he [i.e., Herod] had gathered all the chief priests and scribes of the people together, he demanded of them where Christ should be born."

The same situation could be handled as follows:

"And when [Herod] . . . had gathered. . . ."

f. *Punctuation of quotations.* Commas and periods go inside quotation marks; colons and semicolons go outside. Question marks and exclamation marks go outside quotation marks if they apply to the overall sentence containing the quotation.

> He said, "I'll be there."
> "I'll be there," he said.
> He said, "I'll be there"; but he did not come.
> I know what we must do when we walk through the "valley of the shadow of death": pray.
> He asked, "Why are we here?"
> Did he say, "I'm not coming"?
> Did he ask, "Why are we here?" (*Note*: In this case, both the overall sentence and the quoted matter are questions; use only one question mark, placed as above.)
> He shouted, "I won't go!"
> I will not say "uncle"!

MS 4 • *Plagiarism*

Plagiarism (using someone else's work as if it were one's own) is a serious academic and scholarly offense. Plagiarism may be committed in three ways:

1. Using someone's idea without citing the source.
2. Paraphrasing a source without acknowledging it.
3. Taking words from a source, whether or not the source is cited, without using quotation marks.

Students often commit this third type of plagiarism unwittingly. Remember that paraphrasing means changing all significant words into one's own language and using sentence patterns different from the original. Even if you take only one or two significant words from a source, you must use quotation marks.

Use without documentation only ideas which fall into the category of general information. But if, in relating a widely known idea, you use the words of a specific source, quote and footnote those words.

MS 5 • *Footnotes and Bibliography*

For clarity you should follow a consistent system of making footnotes and bibliography entries. The examples below are based on *The MLA Style Sheet* (2d ed., 1970), a generally accepted authority in literary scholarship. The conventions of documentation are very formalized; you will do well to take great pains with details, even those which to you might seem quite trivial.

a. *The purpose of footnotes.* Footnotes are your means of telling your reader the sources of information and ideas not your own. As a writer of a research paper, you are strictly obligated to give credit to your sources. You need not cite sources for items of general information, as that Columbus discovered the New World in 1492 or that Milton was blind when he composed his later poems.

b. *The placement of footnotes.* Notes can be placed at the bottom of the page or at the end of the paper. Be certain that you understand your instructor's preference.

c. *Footnote numbers.* Notes are numbered consecutively within a paper or within a chapter of a book. The footnote number is raised slightly above the line, with no punctuation.

The footnote number should be placed at the conclusion of a quotation, a paraphrase, or an idea taken from a source. The footnote number comes after all punctuation. (A common error is placing the number just above some mark of punctuation.) If matter from a source extends several lines, then your phrasing should make it clear just how much material is being cited. You could, for example, begin a passage by saying, "Robert Jones argues . . ."; a footnote number several lines later would clearly indicate how much was being credited to Jones.

d. *The spacing of footnotes.* At the bottom of your text, skip a line and then type or draw a line extending about two inches from the left margin. Skip a line and then begin your footnotes. Single space within a footnote; double space between footnotes. Indent the first line of a footnote five spaces; otherwise, a footnote has the same margins as your text. The number of the footnote is raised slightly above the line, just as it is in the text itself.

e. *The purpose of bibliography.* A bibliography indicates the extent of the research which has gone into a paper, it gives a handy recapitulation of items which have been cited in footnotes, and it can serve as an introduction to the literature on the subject of the research paper. If you have done fairly extensive research on a subject, you have become gratefully aware of the usefulness of bibliographies.

f. *Types of bibliographies.* At the top of the first page of your bibliography place a heading describing the kind of listing you make. Of the several kinds of bibliographies, these three would be the most likely in a student paper:

> Works Cited (a list of sources cited in your footnotes)
>
> Works Consulted (a list of all works read, partly or wholly, whether or not they are cited in footnotes)
>
> Selected Bibliography (a list of only the most basic or most important works on a topic)

g. *Arrangement of the bibliography.* Make an alphabetical listing of works, alphabetizing on the basis of the author's last name. If a work is anonymous, use the first word of the title (other than *a, an, the*) to determine alphabetical order. If several authors are listed for a work, put in reverse order only the name of the first one.

The first line of an entry comes to the left margin; all succeeding lines are indented five spaces. Single space within an entry; double space between entries. Do not number items in your bibliography.

h. *Sample footnotes and bibliography entries.* Use the examples below as guides for making footnotes and bibliography entries. Notice that each item is given first as it would appear as a footnote and then as it would be entered in a bibliography. The two forms are given together so that you may readily note the difference between them.

Book with One Author

[3] Rebecca Patterson, *The Riddle of Emily Dickinson* (Boston: Houghton Mifflin Co., 1951), pp. 13-16.

Patterson, Rebecca. *The Riddle of Emily Dickinson.* Boston: Houghton Mifflin Co., 1951.

Book with Two Authors

[1] George Howe and G. A. Harrer, *A Handbook of Classical Mythology* (New York: F. S. Crofts and Co., 1947), p. 129.

Howe, George, and G. A. Harrer. *A Handbook of Classical Mythology.* New York: F. S. Crofts and Co., 1947.

Book, Revised Edition

[6] Thomas Daniel Young, Floyd C. Watkins, and Richmond Croom Beatty, *The Literature of the South,* rev. ed. (Glenview, Ill.: Scott, Foresman and Co., 1968), pp. 219-32.

Young, Thomas Daniel, Floyd C. Watkins, and Richmond Croom Beatty. *The Literature of the South.* Rev. ed. Glenview, Ill.: Scott, Foresman and Co., 1968.

Book with an Editor

[4] D. D. Paige, ed., *The Letters of Ezra Pound, 1907-1941* (New York: Harcourt Brace Jovanovich, Inc., 1950), p. 299.

Paige, D. D., ed. *The Letters of Ezra Pound, 1907-1941.* New York: Harcourt Brace Jovanovich, Inc., 1950.

Book with a Translator

[32] Aristotle, *The Poetics,* trans. Preston H. Epps (Chapel Hill: University of North Carolina Press, 1942), p. 26.

Aristotle. *The Poetics,* trans. Preston H. Epps. Chapel Hill: University of North Carolina Press, 1942.

Chapter in a Book

[11] Cleanth Brooks, "Faulkner the Provincial," *William Faulkner: The Yoknapatawpha Country* (New Haven and London: Yale University Press, 1963), p. 5.

Brooks, Cleanth. "Faulkner the Provincial," *William Faulkner: The Yoknapatawpha Country.* New Haven and London: Yale University Press, 1963, pp. 1-9.

Essay in an Edited Collection

[7] Maurice Kramer, "Sinclair Lewis and the Hollow Center," in *The Twenties, Poetry and Prose: 20 Critical Essays,* ed. Richard E. Langford and William E. Taylor (Deland, Fla.: Everett Press, Inc., 1966), p. 68.

Kramer, Maurice. "Sinclair Lewis and the Hollow Center." *The Twenties, Poetry and Prose: 20 Critical Essays,* ed. Richard E. Langford and William E. Taylor. Deland, Fla.: Everett Press, Inc., 1966, pp. 67-69.

Book in a Series

[13] Nicholas Canaday, Jr., *Melville and Authority*, University of Florida Monographs, Humanities, No. 28 (Gainesville, Fla.: University of Florida Press, 1968), pp. 24-26.

Canaday, Nicholas, Jr. *Melville and Authority*. University of Florida Monographs, Humanities, No. 28. Gainesville, Fla.: University of Florida Press, 1968.

A Work in Several Volumes

[33] Jay Leyda, *The Years and Hours of Emily Dickinson* (New Haven: Yale University Press, 1960), II, 145.

(Note: When a volume number is given, the "p." before the page number is omitted.)

Leyda, Jay. *The Years and Hours of Emily Dickinson*. 2 vols. New Haven: Yale University Press, 1960.

Introduction to a Book

[29] Richard P. Blackmur, "Introduction," *The Art of the Novel: Critical Prefaces by Henry James* (New York: Charles Scribner's Sons, 1934), p. xxi.

Blackmur, Richard P. "Introduction." *The Art of the Novel: Critical Prefaces by Henry James*. New York: Charles Scribner's Sons, 1934, pp. vii-xxxix.

Encyclopedia Article, Unsigned

[17] "Great Britain," *The New International Encyclopedia*, 1903, VIII, 674.

"Great Britain." *The New International Encyclopedia*, 1903, VIII, 644-79.

Encyclopedia Article, Signed

[16] Paul Nettl, "Morris Dance," *Collier's Encyclopedia*, 1965, XVI, 566.

Nettl, Paul. "Morris Dance." *Collier's Encyclopedia*, 1965, XVI, 566.

Unpublished Dissertation

[12]Ima H. Herron, "The Small Town in American Literature" (unpublished doctoral dissertation, Duke University, 1935), p. 24.

Herron, Ima H. "The Small Town in American Literature." Unpublished doctoral dissertation, Duke University, 1935.

Article in a Journal

[42]George Kelly, "Poe's Theory of Beauty," *American Literature*, XXVII (January 1956), 523.

Kelly, George. "Poe's Theory of Beauty." *American Literature*, XXVII (January 1956), 521-36.

Article in Periodical without Volume Number

[8]"How United Fruit Was Plucked," *Business Week*, February 22, 1969, p. 123.

"How United Fruit Was Plucked." *Business Week*, February 22, 1969, pp. 122-24.

Newspaper Article

[42]"Nixon Maneuvers for Talks with Soviets," *The Christian Science Monitor*, February 26, 1969, p. 1.

"Nixon Maneuvers for Talks with Soviets." *The Christian Science Monitor*, February 26, 1969, pp. 1-2.

Published Document or Report

[14]Harold Howe, II, *The People Who Serve Education*, Office of Education Document No. 10059, Department of Health, Education, and Welfare (Washington, D.C., 1969), pp. 9-10.

Howe, Harold, II. *The People Who Serve Education*. Office of Education Document No. 10059. Washington, D.C.: Department of Health, Education, and Welfare, 1969.

Biblical References

[19]Genesis 1:3-6.

Genesis 1:3-6.

(*Note*: Do not use italics for the Bible, the books of the Bible, or the names of other sacred scriptures.)

i. *Footnotes: Second reference.* The first time you cite a source in a footnote, give full information, as in the examples above. Within a paper or within a chapter of a book, second and subsequent references should be made in a clear, shortened form. The exact form to use is determined by a common-sense view of the particular situation. The idea is to be as concise as possible and still to make the identification of the source unmistakable.

[5] Mustin, p. 213.

(Use this simplest way of identifying a source if only one title by this author is cited in your paper.)

[6] Wright, *Mythology*, p. 214.

(Use this form if more than one work by the author is cited in your paper; ordinarily a key word from the title is sufficient.)

MS 6 • *Italics*

In formal writing italics must be used for several purposes. (In print, italic type is slanted, *like this*. The term for regular type is *roman*.) Indicate italics in handwritten or typed material by underlining.

a. *Titles.* Italicize the titles of separate publications (see MS 1, Titles).

The Canterbury Tales, Paradise Lost, Playboy

b. *Ships and vehicles.* Italicize the names of ships, spacecraft, airplanes, trains, and the like.

The Titanic, Apollo 9, The Enola Gay, The Orient Express

c. *Foreign words.* Italicize foreign words and phrases not fully absorbed into English. Avoid guesswork; consult a recent dictionary.

Anglicized words	Words not yet anglicized
coup	*coup de main*
croissant	*Weltschmerz*
junta	*détente*

cabal   *Fuehrer*

concordat   *quod vide*

d. *Words as words.* Italicize references to words as words, letters as letters, and figures as figures.

> *Existence* is a commonly misspelled word.
> His *g* is not clearly formed.
> That *3* is hard to see from here.

e. *For emphasis.* Italicizing for emphasis should be kept to an absolute minimum; the temptation is to depend upon this relatively artificial device rather than upon precise phrasing.

Note the flatness in the following statements.

> I simply *love* the sound of "Ten Years After."
> Country Joe has the most *terrific* singing style.
> The *end* of the affair may be the *beginning* of wisdom.

MS 7 • *Abbreviations*

In formal writing and most college themes you should usually avoid abbreviations. There are, however, many exceptions.

You may use such standard abbreviations as the following.

> titles of address: Dr., Mr.
> academic degrees: M.D., Ph.D.
> organizations generally known by initials: NATO, CIA, SDS
> technical terms generally known by initials: TNT, LSD
> technical terms in a technical context: This engine is capable of 1800 rpm.
> others: B.C. and A.D., St. (meaning saint), A.M. and P.M.

You may use a number of generally accepted abbreviations in your documentation. Although most are from Latin, they are not italicized.

> anon. *anonymous*
> b. *born*
> ca. (circa) *about* (used with dates)
> cf. (confer) *compare*
> ch. *chapter*

chs. *chapters*

comp. *compiled, compiler*

d. *died*

ed. *editor, edition, edited*

eds. *editors, editions*

e.g. (exempli gratia) *for example*

et al. (et alii) *and others*

etc. *and so forth*

ex. *example*

exs. *examples*

f. *and the page following as in* p. 52 f.

ff. *and the pages following*

fn. *footnote*

ibid. (ibidem) *in the same place*

i.e. (id est) *that is*

l. *line*

ll. *lines*

n.d. *no date of publication indicated*

n.p. *no place of publication indicated*

p. *page*

pp. *pages*

pub. *published, publisher*

q.v. (quod vide) *which see*

rev. *review, reviewed, revised, revision*

sic *thus it is* (inserted editorially between brackets to indicate that an error or strangeness in quoted material is accurately reproduced)

trans. *translator, translation, translated*

v. (vide) *see*

vol. *volume*

vols. *volumes*

MS 8 • *Syllabification*

If you must divide a word, use a hyphen at the end of the line to indicate that part of the word is carried over to the next line. Consult a dictionary to resolve any uncertainties.

Do: Divide the word at a break between syllables.

Use a suffix or prefix as the point of division (self-ish, trans-late), if pronunciation allows. Note, however, that the prefix *de* is not the point of division in def-er-ence.

Divide hyphenated words at the point of hyphenation (self-doubt, one-third).

Do Not: Leave a syllable of one letter alone (a-lone).

Divide long words of one syllable (through, fault).

Divide a word at the end of a page.

MS 9 • *Numbers*

In formal writing, spell out numbers which can be written in one or two words (forty, two-thirds, one billion).

Do not begin a sentence with a figure; spell it out or rearrange the sentence.

Use figures for:

dates: June 9, 1961

addresses: 236 West 29th Street

time, with A.M. or P.M.: 12:15 A.M.

decimals: 13.937

technical numbers: mach 8

money, with a dollar sign: $7.20

MS 10 • *Neatness of Manuscripts*

In spite of an instructor's effort at cold impartiality, the appearance of a paper will have some influence. Messiness presents irritating impediments, but legibility and neatness allow the reader to get right to the substance of a paper.

If possible, type your paper; double space your text and leave generous margins.

If you must use handwriting, write neatly on lined, loose-leaf paper (definitely not paper torn out of a spiral notebook); write on alternate lines. Never write on the back of the sheet.

Make corrections neatly. If an erasure would be messy, strike through the error and write the correction above it.

9

Logic and Clarity

Log

Log 1 • Logical Fallacies

The following are the most common of the many abuses of clear thinking. Eliminate them from your thinking and writing.

a. *Hasty generalization*: reaching a conclusion from too little evidence, a major weakness of much writing.

> Both Poe and Coleridge had problems with opium addiction; evidently poets run a great risk of becoming dope fiends. (There is simply not enough evidence for such a sweeping conclusion.)

> Browning and Tennyson wrote dramatic monologues; hence, this form of poetry was replacing the ode as the favorite genre of Victorian poetry. (For such a conclusion one would have to know something about the relative frequency of dramatic monologues in the works of these poets as well as a good deal about other Victorian poets.)

Stereotyping is hasty generalization in which a characteristic observed in several members of a group is taken to be universally applicable to all members of that group. Among those suffering stereotyping have been, for example, college professors, bankers, car salesmen, and racial and ethnic minority groups.

b. *Overgeneralization*: the fallacy of exaggeration.

Qualify broad statements unless you are quite sure that the breadth is warranted by the facts. Tone down conclusions by avoiding such words as "right," "wrong," "true," "never," "always," and "all" unless you are purposefully exaggerating for effect.

Too broad: Nobody understands *Finnegan's Wake*.

Qualified: Probably nobody fully understands *Finnegan's Wake*.

> Bill Tilden was the greatest tennis player who ever lived. (Since no valid comparison among all tennis players is possible, one should more accurately say "Bill Tilden was *one* of the world's greatest tennis players.")

The following are typical of statements that should be modified.

> Never trust anyone over thirty.
>
> All children like Walt Disney movies.
>
> All Southern novelists use Gothic elements in their novels.
>
> None of the generals wants peace.

c. *Abstraction*: the use of words for their vague connotations rather than precise denotations.

Make sure your words have precise meanings. Words like *sincere, courageous, honor, democracy, freedom, justice, brilliant, gorgeous,* and *fabulous* convey little other than vague approval.

> *The Ponder Heart* is a delightful book. (In a theme some criteria of delightfulness would need to be stated precisely.)

> William Gass is a brilliant writer. (Does "brilliant" mean intelligent, skillful, or something else?)

d. *Name calling*: discrediting someone by labeling him with a word that has unfavorable connotations.

Some common derogatory labels are *fascist, communist, reactionary, red, middle class, egghead, red-neck, weirdo, hippy, member of the establishment, rabble-rouser, demagogue, dictator, paternalist, imperialist, racist.*

Most such labels have synonyms that are less prejudiced and less emotionally charged: *conservative* for *reactionary, prudent* for *penny-pinching, Negro moderate* for *Uncle Tom, psychotic* or *demented* for *crazy.*

> John has sold out to the military-industrial complex, become part of the Establishment; he has become so middle class that he probably reads *Reader's Digest* and listens to Lawrence Welk records. (All that this may mean is that John has taken a job with some corporation.)

> John attended the Peace Rally; I always knew he was a hippy weirdo. (The last clause is almost purely emotive.)

e. *Argumentum ad hominem*: an attack on the person rather than his ideas or abilities.

> Oscar Wilde's poetry can't be any good; he was a homosexual who was imprisoned for immorality. (Wilde's sexual practices and his prison record are not really the issue when evaluating his poetry.)

> He could not be an effective judge; he has been married three times. (To discredit someone's ability as a judge, one would have to find grounds more relevant than his marital record.)

> IBM did not hire him for their research program, because he has sideburns and wears blue shirts. (Sideburns and blue shirts are hardly relevant criteria for evaluating someone's capabilities as a researcher.)

f. *Bandwagon*: persuasion by appealing to popular opinion.

Weigh the evidence and form your own opinions, for the majority opinion is not always correct. Almost everyone believed that the *Titanic* was unsinkable; and in the seventeenth century, people smoked for their health.

> Almost everyone at my school believes that ROTC should be retained: therefore, it must be of some value. (The evidence cited does not warrant the conclusion.)

> *Bonanza* must be excellent TV drama, for it has enjoyed high ratings for years. (Popularity need not equal excellence.)

> Rod McKuen's poetry will last; it is tremendously popular. (Popularity does not necessarily mean durability.)

g. *Transfer*: the process of associating the prestige of one person, thing, or idea with another.

Experts out of their own area of competence can be as biased and wrong-minded as anyone else. Great generals are not necessarily well informed in politics, nor is it reasonable to assume that football greats can assess the effectiveness of hair dressing and deodorants any better than you can. Carefully weigh the expertise, experience, and objectivity of any person making a judgment. Any magazine can provide a plethora of advertisements utilizing transfer, as can almost any political campaign. Evidently this is an extremely attractive fallacy.

> I am against regulating offshore oil drilling. After all, the presidents of several of the major oil companies assured us that no irremediable harm had been done by the oil leaks. (These men are somewhat less than disinterested, and their competence in assessing the ecological consequences of the leaks should be questioned.)

Can we doubt his ability to run the university? He has a Ph.D. from Harvard and has written the definitive study of the Rastatt Peasant's Rebellion. (Administrative ability and scholarly competence in history are not necessarily correlated.)

h. *Post hoc, ergo propter hoc* ("after this; therefore because of this"): assuming causation merely because one event follows another.

Causation is very complex; rarely is there a one-to-one relationship. Often the tendency to commit this error is rooted in a desire for easy reasons and oversimplications.

Slavery was the cause of the Civil War. (This was only one of many causes.)

College graduates earn more money than non-college graduates. Therefore, it is just good business to go to college. (Going to college is only one of many causes for the graduates' increased earning potential. Presumably those who begin college are both richer and better informed than the general population; hence they would probably earn more money even without the advantage of a college degree.)

i. *False use of statistics*: unreasonable application of a statistic to a particular individual.

Poor Joan. She has decreased her chances of marriage. Statistics show that fewer female college graduates marry than do women in the general population. (Statistics tell something about a group, not about the individual members of that group.)

He must be well off. He is a doctor and the statistics show that the average income for doctors is over $30,000 a year. (Averages obscure the extremes and hence tell one very little about an individual.)

j. *Non sequitur* ("It does not follow"): stating a conclusion that does not necessarily follow from the evidence provided.

Many of France's leaders failed to get into the best universities. Evidently France is ruled by intellectually inferior men. (Too many other factors are involved for this conclusion to be valid. What about their prep schooling, their social and financial background, their motivation, and the selection criteria of the universities?)

When Melville filled out his marriage certificate, he wrote in his mother's name instead of his wife's; this slip proves he had a severe Oedipus complex. (Such a slip might suggest psychological problems but does not constitute proof.)

Norman Mailer is highly critical of U.S. foreign policy and of big business; he is, thus, anti-American. (No such conclusion is possible from such evidence.)

k. *Begging the question*: assuming a conclusion that needs to be proved or reasoning in a circle.

Poets have more empathy than other people because they understand the feelings of others better. (The reason given is merely a restatement of the conclusion, which itself needs proof.)

"I fight poverty. I work." (The unproved assumption is that people are poor because they refuse to work.)

l. *Guilt (or virtue) by association*: assuming that two things, because they occur together, are invariably linked.

Many great men, Einstein, for instance, did poorly in school. My poor grades, then, can be viewed as a measure of my greatness. (The conclusion is not warranted from the evidence, which says nothing about all the nongreats who did poorly in school nor about the positive basis for Einstein's greatness.)

He must be some sort of a radical; he has a beard, hasn't he? (Not all people with beards are radicals, nor do all radicals have beards.)

m. *Ignoratio elenchi* (arguing off the point): the device of the straw man, in which the question at issue is ignored and an easier question attacked.

The proposed dam on the Colorado is needed. Dams have tamed many wild rivers and have provided a cheap source of electrical power. (The question is a specific dam on a specific river, not dams in general.)

Young men should not avoid the draft. Their elders fought bravely and willingly in World War II. (At issue is not World War II or the action of their elders but the actions of young men in a different situation.)

n. *False dilemma*: the unwarranted limiting of a choice to only two alternatives.

Ronald Firbank was either a madman or a genius. (He could have been both or neither.)

Modern poets are either Romanticists or Classicists. (They could share some qualities of each or even fit more accurately into another classification.)

o. *False analogy*: Analogies are useful for explanation but not for proof.

> We must curtail government's deficit spending. A business soon fails if income does not match expenditures. (Government is not a business. The analogy explains the writer's attitude but does not prove his point.)

> War is necessary, inevitable, and beneficial. Darwin's ideas about the survival of the fittest clearly indicate that this is so. (Nations are not animals; hence biological laws do not necessarily apply.)

> A university cannot be run democratically; a ship's captain does not poll his crew when he makes a decision. (A university is not a ship.)

p. *Poisoning the well*: illegitimately undercutting opposing arguments by providing no grounds for disagreement.

> Of course you do not believe in the Oedipus complex. To accept it would be to admit that you yourself have the problem.

> Your lack of experience and sophistication precludes your ability to understand Yeats' love poetry.

Log 2 • *Ambiguity*

In ordinary themes multiple meanings are distracting and confusing. Ambiguity is exploited, however, for ironical or humorous effects in poetry and certain kinds of essays, and it contributes to the depth and complexity of much modern fiction. Desirable ambiguity is, of course, always purposeful.

Good writers, realizing that words only imperfectly correspond to the thoughts they are trying to express, avoid forcing the reader to choose one of several possible interpretations. One difficulty is that connotations of words differ from person to person; another is that written language is not accompanied with changes of tone, emphasis, and facial expression, and the writer cannot know when the reader is confused. Hence, writing must be clearer and more exact than spoken language. Always reread your writing with a fresh mind. Empathize with the reader.

Ambiguous: *Love Among the Cannibals* is a short novel. (What does "short" mean? It would be clearer if the number of pages were specified.)

Ambiguous: Federico Fellini makes fantastic movies. ("Fantastic" is ambiguous; it could merely indicate approval or it could mean that Fellini deals with fantasy.)

Log 3 • *Comparison*

Comparisons should be between similar items; that is, the items must be commensurate. In comparisons careless errors are frequent.

Ambiguous: Celine's bitterness far exceeds any writer I know.
Clear: Celine has more bitterness than any writer I know.

Ambiguous: An intern makes more money than nurses.
Clear: An intern makes more money than a nurse makes.

Incorrect: The poetry of Robert Frost is more popular than Wallace Stevens.
Correct: The poetry of Robert Frost is more popular than that of Wallace Stevens.

The superlative should be used only when three or more things are being compared.

Incorrect: I read both *Herzog* and *Portnoy's Complaint*, and to me *Herzog* is best.
Correct: I read both *Herzog* and *Portnoy's Complaint*, and to me *Herzog* is better.

Make sure that what is being compared is evident.

> Roethke was the finest poet. (Does this statement mean that he was the finest in the United States, the finest of the twentieth century, or does it simply mean that the writer likes Roethke's poetry?)

Log 4 • *Insufficient detail*

Support generalizations with facts, illustrations, and explanations. A major weakness of much student writing is a failure to back up generalizations and judgments with evidence.

Unconvincing: The English Romantics rejected the art forms of their predecessors in favor of new ones.
Specific: Wordsworth, Coleridge, Keats, and Shelley found other art forms more congenial than those of their predecessors. They wrote few plays, feeling that dramatic restrictions impeded the imagination, and they were little interested in satire, a genre that appeals more to the reason than the imagination. They favored short lyrics to express intense emotion and odes to express serious meditative and philosophical themes.

Log 5 • *Distracting details*

Eliminate all details that do not directly contribute to your purpose. Inconsequential, digressive details, no matter how interesting in themselves, are distracting and confusing.

Digressive: Kingsley Amis, one of the original "Angry Young Men," and one of the few English authors who have been financially successful as an author (he writes for TV), who wrote that hilarious novel of college life, *Lucky Jim*, a brilliant dissection of a young college professor, has been chosen by the estate of Ian Fleming, the creator of James Bond, the spy played so convincingly in the movies by Sean Connery, who has now moved on to acting of more moment, to continue the Bond novels, perhaps because of his writing *The James Bond Dossier*. (The lack of focus amid the multitude of details frustrates the reader.)

Log 6 • *Concreteness*

Be as specific as you possibly can. Do not, for example, write "a corporation manufacturing weapons" if you mean Dow Chemical. Abstractions are never as interesting or as accurate as specifics.

Abstract: He walked strangely.
Specific: He shuffled slowly, as if suffering great fatigue.

Vague: Ross McDonald enjoys outdoor activities.
Specific: Ross McDonald enjoys swimming, sailing, and bird watching.

Avoid weak intensives like *very, so, quite, most, really* and overworked descriptive words like *nice, interesting, lovely, fabulous, fine,* and *awful.* These words often weaken statements.

Log 7 • *Figurative language* (see D 13)

Do not mix figures of speech. Mixed figures are often ludicrous and confusing.

Mixed: If you walk the straight and narrow, you won't get the wind knocked out of your sails. (For consistency and clarity stick to one metaphor or the other, walking or sailing, or abandon metaphor entirely.)

Mixed: Although Walter Mitty outwardly toed the mark and kept his nose to the grindstone, inwardly he was as restless as a caged lion.

Figures of speech are properly used to give statements more intensity and vividness. Trite, outworn metaphors cannot do this. Figurative language should be fresh, accurate, and relevant. The following figures meet none of these requirements and should be avoided in writing and in speech.

burning questions	dumb like a fox
broad daylight	run like a deer
last but not least	in a nutshell
few and far between	beyond the shadow of a doubt
hit the nail on the head	on the brink
see the handwriting on the wall	burn the midnight oil
pretty as a picture	easier said than done
sell like hotcakes	rude awakening
method in madness	a day of reckoning
fall short	sink or swim
leave no stone unturned	sneaking suspicion
run it up the flagpole	the straight and narrow
get some feedback	beady eyes
with bated breath	

10

Glossary of Usage

Gl

This glossary is a list of expressions which most frequently give trouble in student writing. Regular use of a dictionary will be helpful in eliminating such errors.

accept, except
   accept: to consent or to receive
   except: to rule out or to exclude

adapt, adopt
   adapt: to make suitable alterations or adjustments in
   adopt: to take as one's own

affect, effect
   affect: to influence
   effect: (verb) to bring into being
            (noun) the result or consequence of an event or thing

aggravate: to make worse or to intensify. Often used colloquially for *to irritate* or *to anger*.

allusion, illusion
   allusion: an indirect reference to a thing
   illusion: a fantasy or false impression

almost, most
   Almost is an adverb; *most*, an adjective

Acceptable: *Almost* every important rock group was at Woodstock.

Acceptable: *Most* contemporary poets work in universities.

Incorrect: The larger owls eat *most* everything.

already, all ready
>   *already*: previously or prior to a given time
>   *all ready*: fully prepared

>> He has *already* passed his draft physical.
>> The Senate is *all ready* to consider limiting presidential powers.

alright: a misspelling of *all right*

all together, altogether
>   *all together*: in a group or in harmony
>   *altogether*: entirely or with reference to everything

among, between
>   *among*: used with reference to three or more
>   *between*: used with reference to two

amount, number
>   *amount*: applies to quantity or mass
>   *number*: applies to things which may be counted or perceived separately

ante-, anti-
>   *ante-*: a prefix meaning prior to
>   *anti-*: a prefix meaning against or in opposition to

any one, anyone
>   *anyone*: an indefinite pronoun
>   *any one*: with reference to any individual

>> *Anyone* over eighteen may attend an X-rated film.
>> Can *any one* of you accurately predict the fluctuation of the stock market?

a while, awhile
>   *a while*: noun phrase, meaning a short period of time
>   *awhile*: an adverb

>> For *a while* the migration was delayed by strong winds.
>> Thousands of warblers rested *awhile* on the sandy promontory.

bad, badly
> *bad*: an adjective; may be used with linking verbs
> *badly*: must be used in formal writing as the adverb

With linking verb: I feel *bad*.
Incorrect: He played *bad*.
Improved: He played *badly*.

beside, besides
> *beside*: indicates position or location
> *besides*: means *in addition to*

between (see *among*)

but
> In the sense of *only*, *but* should be used without any other negative.

Incorrect: Psychologically, Poe doesn't develop *but* one mood—terror.
Acceptable: Psychologically, Poe develops *but* one mood—terror.

> Other words with negative force: *hardly, only, scarcely*.

capital, capitol
> *capital*: a city
> *capitol*: a building

complement, compliment
> *complement*: that which completes a thing
> *compliment*: a favorable or praising statement

connotation, denotation
> *denotation*: the literal meaning
> *connotation*: the associated meanings attached to a word

House and *home* have the same *denotation*, but *home* has a more favorable *connotation*.

continual, continuous
> *continual*: of frequent occurrence
> *continuous*: without interruption or cessation

could of
> Incorrectly used in the sense of *could have*.

council, counsel
>   *council*: an advisory or legislative body
>   *counsel*: an advisor or an opinion

criterion (singular), criteria (plural)

denotation (see *connotation*)

differ from, differ with
>   One differs *from* a thing, *with* a person or argument.

disinterested, uninterested
>   *Disinterested* suggests objectivity; *uninterested* indicates indifference.

due to
>   Avoid using *due to* as an introduction to an adverbial phrase.

Flawed: Due to public outrage, Lawrence's novel *The Rainbow* was suppressed.
Improved: Because of public outrage, Lawrence's novel *The Rainbow* was
   suppressed.

elicit, illicit
>   *elicit*: to draw forth or bring to light
>   *illicit*: illegal or proscribed

effect (see *affect*)

emigrate, immigrate
>   *emigrate*: to leave a country
>   *immigrate*: to come to and settle in a country

eminent, imminent
>   *eminent*: of high station
>   *imminent:* impending, about to happen

everyone, every one
>   *everyone*: an indefinite pronoun
>   *every one*: every single person

except (see *accept*)

explicit, implicit

explicit: clearly stated
implicit: suggested but not openly stated

farther, further
    farther: with reference to actual distance
    further: with reference to abstract or figurative relationships

      The Aleutian Islands extend *farther* into the ocean than the Florida Keys.
      Methods to combat automobile pollution need *further* development.

fewer, less
    Use *fewer* to refer to numbers or things which may be perceived individually,
      less to refer to things not perceptible as individual units.

      Unchecked hunting has reduced the whooping crane population to *fewer*
      than one hundred birds.
      The later poetry of Dylan Thomas is *less* vital than his earlier work.

further (see *farther*)

good
    Avoid using *good* as an adverb.

Adverbial: Goldstein fought *good* against Hudkins until the seventh round.
Improved: Goldstein fought *well* against Hudkins until the seventh round.

good and
    Do not use in the sense of *very*.

Adverbial: A horse finishing the Grand National is *good and* tired.
Improved: A horse finishing the Grand National is *extremely* tired.

hanged, hung
    With reference to the method of execution, use *hanged* as past tense and past
      participle. Use *hung* in all other references.

      They *hung* the mist net carefully across the path.
      They Hanged My Saintly Billy.

hardly (see *but*)

illicit (see *elicit*)

illusion (see *allusion*)

immigrate (see *emigrate*)

implicit (see *explicit*)

imply, infer
> One *implies* a meaning in his own statement; one *infers* a meaning in the statement of someone else.

> Marvell *implies* an ironic attitude throughout the poem.
> One can *infer* from Marvell's poem a sense of comic urgency.

imminent (see *eminent*)

infer (see *imply*)

ingenious, ingenuous
> *ingenious*: of great intellectual or imaginative quality
> *ingenuous*: naive or innocent; artless or forthright

inside of
> The *of* is unnecessary in statements like this:

> The prism lenses are placed inside *of* the barrel of the binocular.

> Avoid *inside of* in the sense of "within."

Informal: John Carlos can run one hundred yards *inside of* 9.5 seconds.
Improved: John Carlos can run one hundred yards within 9.5 seconds.

irregardless
> Nonstandard. Use *regardless*.

its, it's
> *Its* is possessive; *it's* is a contraction of *it is*.

kind of, sort of, type of
> Be certain to include the *of* in phrases like the following:

> > that kind of boy
> > those kinds of apples
> > a strange sort of horse
> > a wild type of woman.

later, latter
> *Later* refers to time; *latter*, to the second of two things.

less (see *fewer*)

let's
> A contraction of *let us*, often used in the redundant expression *let's us*.

liable
> Formally used to mean *legally responsible*; often used informally to mean *likely*.

Informal: Political conditions in Belfast are not *liable* to improve suddenly.

Improved: Political conditions in Belfast are not *likely* to improve suddenly.

like, as
> Use *like* as a preposition, but not as a conjunction.

Preposition: The villanelle, *like* the Petrarchan sonnet, is seldom used by modern poets.

Conjunction: *Like* he had been warned, he soon discovered the intricacies of the experiment.

Improved: *As* he had been warned, he soon discovered the intricacies of the experiment.

lots, a lot
> *Lots* is plural and therefore cannot take the singular article.

maybe, may be
> *Maybe* means perhaps; *may be* is a verb.

most (see *almost*)

most of
> Incorrectly used in the sense of *must have*.

notorious
> Use in the sense of *unfavorable fame*. Do not confuse with *notable* and *famous*, which have favorable connotations.

nowhere near
> Do not use for *not nearly*.

off of
> The *of* is unnecessary and informal.

only (see *but*)

outside of
> The *of* is unnecessary in a statement like this:

> Even outside *of* the marsh, the call of bitterns still could be heard.

Informal: The black-whiskered vireo is not found in any state *outside of* Florida.

Improved: The black-whiskered vireo is not found in any state *except* Florida.

pass time, pastime

> I will *pass time* awkwardly in prison.
> Bridge is a vicious *pastime*.

personal, personnel

> The *threnody* is a very *personal* poetic form.
> The *personnel* of The Who are all highly skilled musicians.

phenomenon (singular), phenomena (plural)

principal, principle
> *principal*: of the first rank
> *principle*: a truth or standard

real
> Avoid as an adverb.

Adverbial: Wittgenstein is a *real* complex philosopher.
Improved: Wittgenstein is an *extremely* complex philosopher.

reason is because
> Avoid. Use *reason is that*.

> The *reason* we won *is that* we had eight high trumps.

respectfully, respectively
> *respectfully*: deferentially, with esteem
> *respectively*: in the order of items previously named

scarcely (see *but*)

so
> Avoid as an intensive.

Informal: A background in linguistics is *so* helpful in understanding Whorf's discoveries.

Improved: A background in linguistics is *very* helpful in understanding Whorf's discoveries.

> *So* may be used to introduce clauses.

>> Poets use symbols *so that* the complexity of reality can be fully rendered.

someone, some one
> *Someone* is the indefinite pronoun.

>> *Someone* is always injured during riots.

>> If *some one* of you will not act responsibly, the problem of mercury pollution will continue.

sort of (see *kind*)

stationary, stationery
> *stationary*: adjective, meaning in a fixed position
> *stationery*: noun, meaning writing paper

statue, stature, statute
> *statue*: a piece of sculpture
> *stature*: physical structure or build
> *statute*: a law

such
> A weak and self-defeating intensive.

Weak: It is such a fine epigram.

Improved: It is a fine epigram.

suppose to
> Often erroneously used for *supposed to*.

sure and
> An informal usage for *sure to*.

than, then
    Than is used in comparisons; *then*, to refer to time.

    I enjoyed Dylan more *then than* I do now.

theirself, theirselves
    Nonstandard for *themselves*.

there, their, they're
    there: adverb or expletive subject

    There are numerous recondite allusions in Pound's Cantos.

    their: possessive pronoun
    they're: contraction of they are

try and
    Informal for *try to*.

type (see *kind*)

uninterested (see *disinterested*)

use to
    Often erroneously used for *used to*.

way, ways
    Do not use *ways* in a singular sense.

Erroneous: "It's a long *ways* to Tipperary."
Improved: "It's a long *way* to Tipperary."
Acceptable: The *ways* of the Shaman seem strange to us.

where . . . at
    Omit the redundant *at*.

Redundant: Conservationists know *where* the chief source of water pollution is *at*.
Improved: Conservationists know *where* the chief source of water pollution is.

you
    Avoid *you* as the indefinite pronoun in formal writing. Use a third-person pronoun (e.g., one, someone) or name the kind of person being referred to: *the student, the reader*.

you all
    Acceptable only in the plural sense.

Index

Numbers (*cont.*)
and commas, 46
compound, 52
in manuscripts, 87

Objects, 4-5
direct, 4, 6, 33
of preposition, 5, 6-7, 33
of verbals, 33
of verbs, 2
Objective case, 32, 33
Objective complement, 40
Obscenities, 64
one, 30
or, 3
otherwise, 25, 29
Outline, of library paper, 73-74
Overgeneralization, 88-89
Overstatement, 68-69

Pagination, 76
Pamphlets, titles of, 75
Paragraph(s):
argumentative, 15, 16
coherence of, 17-18
concluding, 23-24
contrast in, 19-20
expository, 15-16
introductory, 23-24
length and variety, 18
narrative, 15, 16
organization of, 18-23
types of, 15-16
unity in, 17
Parallel construction, 73
Parallelism, 12
Parenthesis, 49-50, 56-57
Parenthetical elements, and commas, 45
Participles, 2, 5
Parts of speech, 1, 2
Passive voice, 11, 14
Periodical guide, 71
Periods, 43, 78
Person, avoid shifts in, 37
Personification, 68-69
Phrases, 5-6
absolute, 6
adjectival, 5

Phrases (*cont.*)
adverbial, 6
elliptical, 38
gerund, 5
infinitive, 5
introductory verbal, 44
as modifiers, 3
noun, 5
prepositional, 4, 5, 39, 44
verb, 5
Plagiarism, 78
Plays, titles of, 75
Plurals, 2, 41, 53-54 (*see also* Agreement)
Poetry, 76
"Poisoning the well" logic, 93
Possessive case, 32-34 *passim*, 51
Predicate, 2
Predicate adjective, 4
Predicate nouns, 4, 28
Prefixes, 58
Prepositions, 1, 4, 5, 42
Pronouns, 41
agree with antecedent, 30-31
in apposition, 34
defined, 1
personal, forms of, 32
reference, 31-32
reflexive, 33
relative, 4, 6, 7
as subject, 2
Punctuation, 43-50
brackets, 50
colon, 47-48
comma, 44-47
dash, 49
exclamation point, 48
parentheses, 49-50
period, 43
question mark, 48
quotation marks, 49
semicolon, 47
of sentence, 1

Question mark, 48, 78
Questions, 2
Quotation marks, 49
and punctuation, 78
for titles, 75